DIFFERENCE IS NOT DEFICIT

A Community Vision for Special Education

Dr. Bibinaz Pirayesh

HEINEMANN | Portsmouth, NH

Acknowledgments:
Front Cover Image: © Sakchai Vongsasiripat/Getty Images

Author Photo: Courtesy of WASIOfaces.com

Figure 1.3: "What Is Positionality?" created by Dr. Meagan Pollock, Engineered Organizations. Courtesy of the author. www.drmp.co/positionality.

Figure 2.2: "Some Basic Feelings We All Have" from *Nonviolent Communication: A Language of Life* by Marshall B. Rosenberg. Copyright © 2015 PuddleDancer Press. Reproduced by permission of PuddleDancer Press (Grant Meiji Stewart, Publisher).

Acknowledgments continue on page 146.

Library of Congress Cataloging-in-Publication Data
Names: Pirayesh, Bibinaz author
Title: Difference is not deficit : a community vision for special education / by Bibinaz Pirayesh.
Description: Portsmouth, NH : Heinemann, [2025] | Includes bibliographical references.
Identifiers: LCCN 2025021310 | ISBN 9780325178899
Subjects: LCSH: Students with disabilities—United States | Special education—United States | Inclusive education—United States | Educational equalization—United States
Classification: LCC LC4031 .P497 2025
LC record available at https://lccn.loc.gov/2025021310

Printed in the U.S.A. on acid-free paper

ISBN-13: 978-0-325-17889-9

4500918921 r10.25

FOR MY MOTHER,

WHO TAUGHT ME TO

LOVE JUSTICE.

FOR THE CHILDREN OF GAZA,

WHO TAUGHT ME

WHAT INJUSTICE TRULY COSTS.

CONTENTS

CHAPTER 1

UNDERSTANDING DEFICIT PARADIGMS

I became an educator through my own disillusionment with the education system. With a K–12 education received across three countries—elementary school in Iran, middle school in the United States, and high school in Canada—I started college convinced that schooling was broken across the globe. Higher education was no different. I soon learned that all schools follow the same model: the goal is not growing or learning but is instead finding your place in the capitalist machinery and getting to business. For me, it felt wrong—like I was being taught to succeed in a world I didn't believe in. It was deeply unsettling, and although like everyone else I conformed and performed well in school, that unease never left me. I wanted to know why.

Despite its efforts to indoctrinate me, the same education system also ignited my revolutionary spirit. The more the system pushed me, the more I dug in my heels and pushed back. In its refusal to let me be myself, in its insistence that I submit to its thinking and its needs, it pushed me more toward a quest for my authentic self and answers to my burning and unanswered questions.

VOCABULARY

An **educational therapist** is a professional who provides individualized support and training to students with learning disabilities. They integrate cognitive neuroscience, educational strategies, and therapeutic approaches and help learners with skill remediation, accommodations, and self-advocacy. Educational therapists also collaborate closely with families and schools to help create a supportive learning environment tailored to each student's unique needs.

When I first started work as an educational therapist, a field I knew little about, I was in a moment of complete exhaustive collapse. I had finished a graduate program in cognitive science and developmental psychology, once again disappointed by an "education" that had this time buried me so deeply in debt that I wasn't sure how I would get out of it. I took a job that I was told I was overqualified for and that paid about the same as a barista, mostly to get off my family's couch, but also because it promised "training." By then I had spent years in academia trying to understand my own disenchantment with school despite my love of learning. I had approached the issue from multiple perspectives: neuroscience, cognitive science, developmental psychology, educational philosophy. Nowhere was I able to find the answers I sought. Yet I still believed in the power of schooling and in the sacred space between teacher and student, a space that had saved me many times despite my general disappointment with my educational experiences. Maybe, I thought, that's where I should have looked all along. Maybe the answers were exactly in that space. And they were.

At the time I started, I had never worked with students with learning disabilities. I had no personal experience with learning disabilities and, given my strong beliefs in the impact of environmental factors—parenting, socioeconomic status, trauma, etc.—I wasn't even sure I believed in many of the diagnoses given to children.

In a way you could say I felt uncomfortable with my profession from the start. My first "client," Andrew, was a sixteen-year-old boy with ADHD. His parents were divorced and his mother had remarried and had a new child with a man I could tell Andrew feared. Though I never tested him, Andrew seemed to me a gifted child. He was also failing all his classes and his mother was convinced that his new ADHD diagnosis and medication, alongside therapy with me, would help him succeed at his very challenging all-boys high school in Los Angeles. The plan was for him to go on to NYU, his mother's alma mater, and study film, which had been her dream. This was essentially Andrew's goal: to bear the burden and realize the dream of his mother's unlived life, to use Carl Jung's famous quote. The problem was that I wanted to talk to Andrew about *him*. I wanted to know more about his fear of his wealthy stepfather and his feelings about his own father, his parents' divorce, and his little sister, whom he seemed to adore even more than her father did. It seemed to me that there was so much to process in their circumstances that any brain would find it overwhelming, especially one as deeply intuitive as Andrew's. Perhaps we should start there, I thought, not with the ADHD diagnosis, and we should leave the path open, not clearly ending at NYU.

It wasn't long before I had a whole roster of children whose academic lives and learning profiles I was charged with "fixing" but whose personal stories felt so important to their well-being and, in my youthful and inexperienced but also intuitive view, absolutely tied to their academic success. I was frustrated that despite the privilege of working with kids in such an intimate one-on-one way, I was still forced to adhere to the forces of the larger system (in this case the parents* but also the school and cultural norms), and if I objected or wanted to change course, the parents would resist. This is one of

*In this book, "parents" is used to refer to those in the role of primary caregiver or acting parent.

the most difficult aspects of working with children. The child is the nominal client, but the parents are in charge (and in my work are the ones literally paying for the service), so they are the real customers. And somehow the capitalist adage that the customer is always right still applies, even though the parents have technically brought in an expert to figure out what isn't working.

For the first few years, I wondered if I was the problem. Perhaps if I were a clinical psychologist, if I had a doctoral degree, they would be more willing to listen to me. I did have a master's degree from the same Ivy League school many of these parents wanted me to help get their children into, but since I had already walked that path, I knew there were no answers there. Still, I doubted my own intuitive knowing and wondered if the problem was that I still wasn't educated and expert enough. As I worked more in the field, however, and got to observe the dynamics with psychologists and bigger and better experts, I came to appreciate the freedom my lesser position as an educator allowed me. Under the guise of academic work, I was able to informally engage in therapeutic work that no therapist was doing. I would make home visits. Being in the spaces where the kids lived, I would get to see them interact with their siblings, their pets, their parents, their nannies. I would get to observe and feel everything, from the major meltdowns to the minor slights between parent and child that explained their whole world and dynamics. And I would do so quietly, never letting on how much I saw, how much I understood, and how much I planned to use that understanding in my work with the children.

Occasionally, my students would have a meltdown. Sometimes I would, too (I had learned to make my meltdowns quiet). One often thinks of injustice in terms of oppression and war fronts and prisons. But as a survivor of oppression and wars and revolutions, I would say some of the deepest injustices, the most heinous acts of psychological abuse with the most profound and long-lasting impact, happen in the living room of your average family.

I used writing as a tool to help me manage my quiet meltdowns. I knew from the times they happened, when I could no longer stay silent and had to point out to a parent that "no, actually, you're the problem" (the backlash being either getting fired or being silenced and shamed), that if I wanted to keep the relationship with the child and continue to help, I had to survive, like they were surviving. I was in my late twenties then and still processing my own traumas, but even today, when I would feel far more confident saying "no, you're the problem," I know better than to voice it. Whatever oppressive system a person is in, staying connected to it is essential to effect change. No one understands a system better than those within it, which is why resistance is sometimes most effective from the inside.

Even today, I try to imagine how the world would be, what our education and mental health systems would be, if we were free to speak our truths. None of us are. Whether our "bosses" are school administrators or parents, we all have to swallow truths for the sake of professionalism. But what's ironic—and tragic—in our professions is that we are expected to teach this masking, to enforce this brainwashing of children who are still brave enough to speak up. If you work with kids who especially struggle to mask, like I do, your job becomes that much more brutal.

When Andrew did get into NYU—a success I was told reflected well on my efforts—I was more worried about him leaving his family than he was. He wasn't ready to move across the country and take on the responsibility of life on his own, and we both knew it. His stepfather saw this reluctance as a failure of his character, an inability to step up and be a man. His mother simply saw it as non-negotiable. We hadn't worked so hard for two years to get him in only for him to not go. She saw it as my job to convince him and to get him ready. I did everything I could think of to protect Andrew. I tried to reason with his parents, to explain why the move would be a shock to his system. I described what I saw, the potential for falling apart, for depression, for drugs, for dropping out. They only wanted to know if I was withholding information about his drug use. I wasn't. I even did the work of mapping out an alternate route: a community college close to home for one to two years and a slow transition. They found the idea preposterous when he had demonstrated the ability to gain acceptance to NYU. The more I pushed and pleaded, the more they pulled back, and I found myself so enraged, so righteously angry at the young age of twenty-eight, that I gave them an ultimatum. I would have none of it. I would not work with him remotely as they had asked. I would not continue to push him when I felt so deeply that it wasn't right and, even more important, when he was voicing such reluctance. "He's just scared," they told me, "and he needs to learn to face himself." To me, Andrew's voicing his fear and his inability to navigate the change *was* him facing himself. But I was thanked for my services and given a big bonus, and I never heard from Andrew or his family again.

Today, I would handle Andrew's situation differently. I would concede. I would do as his parents asked and work with him remotely. I would do everything in my power to remain a support in his life, because if he crashed, it would be more beneficial for him to have me as a support than not. At the time I struggled with this. How could I charge money to do something I didn't believe in? How could I side with his parents "against" him? I felt my integrity was on the line. But mostly, my frustration was a naive sense that I could beat the machine. There was a kind of egotism in believing that, armed with integrity and truth, I could change Andrew's fate, his parents, their psychology, the larger culture, and all the forces that construct our world. But what I also understood incorrectly at the time was my own power. While I was already beginning to see the brokenness of our modality, I couldn't see that despite that, within the field of education, individuals still have space to exercise their power, not just to help young people but to slowly change the system from within.

If you feel oppressed and suffocated in your work, you are correct. Our entire setup is against humanity. And while many of us are not conscious of it, our job is to teach the next generation how to be okay feeling oppressed and how to accept their own dehumanization. This is both cruel and essential to survival. I try to remember this when working with parents who are pushing their children too hard or with teachers who are being unreasonably strict with their class rules and expectations. We do have to prepare the next generation for surviving in an abusive, dehumanizing culture. But there is also space for change. This is what I learned in those rooms where I could not speak. Within these same structures of oppression, each of us has small slivers of opportunity to push for change. The key to being a good therapist or teacher is to keep our attention there.

As I write this book, schools across the country continue to debate curriculum and book censorships. I think the impact of the shift first hit me when I heard about a school district in Texas removing *The Diary of a Young Girl* (Frank 1995) from its shelves. I had first read Anne Frank and learned about her life when I was in the seventh grade. At that point, my family had only been in the United States for about a year and a half, and English class was hard. We had just finished reading *Romeo and Juliet*, which even my mom and her dictionary couldn't help me decode at night. Reading something written by a teenager, in far simpler language, was a welcome reprieve. I still struggled to comprehend the text, but I remember reading it eagerly. I had grown up in a country where some questioned the Holocaust entirely. I had learned from my parents and other members of my family that the Holocaust had in fact happened and the Jewish people had suffered greatly in WWII. Yet I had also seen some religious and political programs—the main types of shows on Iranian television in the late 1980s—questioning the legitimacy of the Holocaust. Now here was Anne giving a firsthand account. I remember naively wondering if those denying the Holocaust had actually read her diary and whether they might change their minds if they did. But mostly I remember how Anne's fear, which leaped off the pages despite all the words I couldn't understand, was palpable, real, and familiar.

While growing up in Iran meant that I could never naively believe in America's great promise of democracy and freedom, even my most critical mind could never have predicted that I would see a day when *The Diary of a Young Girl* would be the target of a ban attempt in American schools. In fact, since the summer of 2020, and the aftermath of the murder of George Floyd, I regularly wake up in the mornings, look at the news, and wonder if this is in fact the same America I have lived in for the last three-plus decades. What has been especially surprising as an educator is the sudden intense interest in education and curriculum, something that I have never known the average American parent, or the culture at large, to care much about. What is being taught and how was always a central question of national debate in the Islamic Republic of Iran. An entire department of censorship, the Ministry of Ershad, existed just to make decisions about what we were allowed to know and to learn as children. I remember my aunt, who was a university professor, writer, and translator, being enraged about one of her correspondences with the Ministry of Ershad because they would not allow her to translate the word *bottle*. It implied alcohol use, they had informed her in a formal letter, even though the original text was referring to a bottle of water, and she therefore had to take it out. On another occasion, they wanted her to take out a description of the leg of a table because the depiction of its curvy shape was too erotic.

In Iran, every stroke of a teacher's pen, every word uttered, was a potential radical act of revolution, with sometimes harrowing consequences. This was in stark contrast to the way teachers were seen, essentially as babysitters, in American culture. On the ever-solid hierarchical ladder of capitalism, teachers seemed to occupy a pretty low rung. "Those who can't do, teach" the American saying goes—something one would never hear in Iran because there, we had come to understand that in indoctrinating or emancipating the minds of children, teachers are *the* most important agents in society.

This book hinges on three arguments (shown in Figure 1.1). The first is that teaching is political, and teachers are the most important leaders in a society because they shape, more than any others, the political consciousness of the next generation. Second, to do this mindfully, educators must first become politically and critically conscious themselves. The final argument of this book is that there exists in every classroom a window into

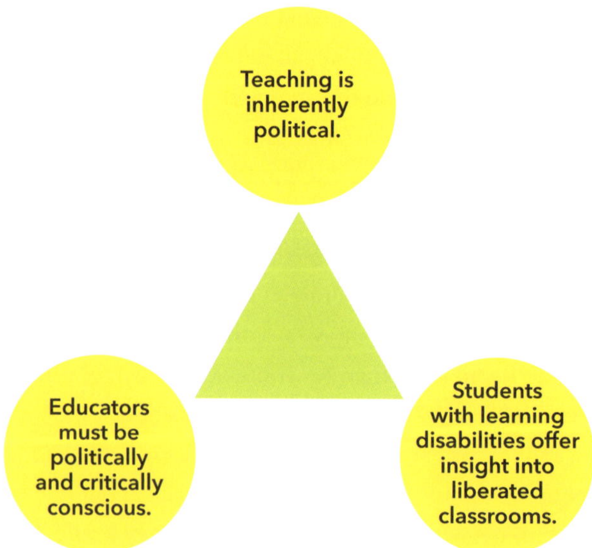

FIGURE 1.1

the necessary changes we must make, a path and a guide toward the emancipation of our classrooms and our curriculums, a light that is provided by the students we often ignore: those with learning disabilities. It's often the ones who don't fit the most that teach us the most about what we need to change. Every teacher is capable of and must step into that role, whatever the circumstances of their work.

THE MEDICALIZATION OF EDUCATION

When I began my private practice, the researcher in me was intrigued to have the chance to watch kids in their element, to observe them as they attempted to learn and solve problems, to understand how their minds slowly grew and developed. In the tradition of my heroes like Jean Piaget (1952) and John Holt (1964), I imagined a practice in which I created a space that allowed the wisdom of nature to reveal itself to me. How do we in fact learn? What is innate? What is necessary in the environment? I had a million questions, big and small, and I felt honored at the opportunity to work with every student.

But it wasn't long before I began to feel the intrusive push, even in my own private setting where I had complete control over how I wanted to do things, to listen less and to act more. I was inundated by ads and conferences and colleagues and networking groups and the newest developments in the field. Parents sometimes fed into this even more than professionals, demanding to know the latest and greatest tools and even trying to dictate what I did in my practice.

Unfortunately, often the most cutting-edge "tools" in the field were all about testing and assessing kids to more accurately identify the problems in them, only to then prescribe ways to "fix" and treat those problems. It was as if we were not at all concerned with what the children brought to the table, what their actual experiences were, or what they had to teach us. Rather, it was what we could imprint on them and how we could fix them that was the undercurrent of the field. Every child was measured against this picture of an "ideal student" that did not take into account circumstance, context, or culture—a description that could be easily applied to white supremacy.

It was not until years later that I came to realize this anxiously driven need to diagnose and fix is the result of an intentional and persistent effort that has long plagued American education. Despite the rhetoric about a holistic approach that teaches the whole child, it is the effort to make education more scientific and therefore more legitimate that has historically controlled the narrative around schooling in America (Au 2011; Biesta 2010; Darder 2017; Kliebard 2004; Kirylo 2013); while this is at times a "hidden curriculum" (Jackson 1968, 183), often it is made quite explicit in the field. There are entire movements today lobbying for education to copy the medical model, relying more on data, diagnosis, and evidence-based approaches rather than relationships, observation, and scaffolding. (It is important to note that the link between medicine and education seems to be psychology, a field that has long tried to establish itself as a science, but one that I will later argue is actually based on subjective interpretation rather than the objective facts it hopes to convince us it exemplifies.) I see this every day in my practice as ordinary children who need good teaching more than anything else are subjected to lengthy clinical tests usually reserved for extreme cases (such as brain lesions) in order to learn how best to teach them. One could argue that our entire approach to

White supremacy is not just an ideology held by individuals–it's a structuring logic that organizes society culturally, politically, and economically. It normalizes white ways of being, knowing, and governing as superior, often invisibly, to concentrate power in the hands of a privileged few. This system isn't about individual white people being bad; it's about how racial hierarchies are upheld to preserve power. Like all systems of supremacy, it uses social categories–race, gender, class–to divide and control. Whiteness is the tool, not the root. Even those who benefit from it are shaped by it. The goal is to challenge the system, not to assign personal blame.

standardized teaching also grows from this movement, as if there is a way to essentialize the messy, complex, and often illusive magic that happens in a classroom to steps and scripts and data. All this to make education more systemic and clinical, like medicine.

The irony, of course, is that most doctors today would tell you the current Western medical model is broken and extremely limited by the testing and measurement requirements often put in place by insurance companies rather than clinicians. Most doctors would probably also say they wish they could spend more time getting to know their patients, meeting them where they are at, understanding their environment and their feelings, thoughts, and needs. Western modern medicine fails on all these fronts, and both patients and caregivers suffer as a consequence. So why would we want education to follow a broken model?

Critical educator Antonia Darder unpacks the impact and cost of these so-called reform movements on BIPOC children specifically. In her book *Culture and Power in the Classroom* (2012), she argues that the American education system is so intentionally set up to reinforce social control and inequity that we not only fall short of our democratic ideals, but rather we actually hold in place inequalities tied to class, gender, sexuality, and ability. We do this, she and many others have shown, primarily through overtesting racialized children in schools (Au 2011; Lipman 2004; Darder 2012). Additionally, the now normalized obsession with testing and assessment in education is linked to the US socioeconomic landscape. Every time the economy is depressed, we suddenly begin to hear the rhetoric about the failures of public schooling and the need for new reforms (Lipman 2004; Duncan-Andrade and Morrell 2008; Molnar 1996). These new reforms in turn somehow always turn to a for-profit model (I admit fields like mine are part of this for-profit engine where only those students who have the means are allowed to access the science-based resources), giving educators a reminder about the importance of how things are in the "real world," which ironically is always limited to capitalist economics where competition rules supreme and what counts is the bottom line.

It's important to note here that historically in the West, science has long been used as an excuse to expand apartheid and genocide. If you have ever wondered about the similarities, for example, between schools and prisons—similar architectures, similar schedules, similar foods, similar "recess" times outside between long periods of physical constriction, similar surveillance and rules of conduct, similar hierarchical authority figures and structures, even similar buses—this is not accidental. Institutionalization of the human body and spirit is big business in America. And whether you look at it in terms of the school-to-prison pipeline or the school-to-workforce pipeline, what you will discover is the prominent role science and psychology-based education play in fueling these pipelines. The statistics around the number of inmates with learning disabilities is mind boggling (Maruschak et al. 2021; Wang 2022). For a while, there was an infamous graphic in education circles depicting how prisons determine the number of beds they'll need based on fourth-grade national reading test scores. Whether that graphic is based on fact or not, there is no question that we use science and diagnosis as a means of societal control. Education historians have done a beautiful job showing how testing, assessment, and evidence-based and "scientific" curriculums are directly linked to economic forces, with poor children, immigrant children, and children of color being the product teachers must prepare for the workforce and those with learning differences being the collateral damage of an ableist system that labels anyone who cannot produce as disabled (Gould 1981).

Neuroscience and Inequity

The new inspiration in the field of neuroscience and brain-based approaches to education claims that by studying the brain, we can inform teachers how to teach better. This is done primarily by placing the disability inside the brain or body of the "patient." This is in direct contradiction to what disability studies, history, and advocacy tell us about recognizing that it is in fact the culture and the environment that disables, not the diagnosis (Jackson 1968; Linton 1998; Shakespeare 2006). This is also in direct contradiction to thousands of years of human history, science, and tradition before empiricism in which mental health was seen and dealt with more as an issue of human consciousness and spirituality (Ellenberger 1970; Kirmayer and Minas 2000; Nielsen 2012). But because the spiritual parts of humans cannot be observed and measured in the ways empiricism requires, we have devised a system that places the problem in the body of the person, and, fueled by Christian ideology, explains it away as God's will, hence creating shame and stigma around it. That we do not stop to ask if we are asking the right questions, that we may be missing whole aspects of the human being in our focus on only that which can be observed, seem not unfortunate shortcomings but deliberate design, one that is deeply intertwined with the politics and economics of selling cures instead of promoting different (free) approaches to healing our minds and our hearts.

I want to emphasize here that I am not against the use of different programs or even the scientific pursuit of discovering or inventing more effective remediative tools. My point is not that empirical science is not a useful tool or that we should teach solely based on feelings and intuition. But as someone who has been studying the intersection of neuroscience and education for decades, I can tell you, first, that neuroscience as a field of knowledge is still at the very early stages of its development and therefore still has very little to contribute to a field as historically robust as education (unfortunately this is not the rhetoric that sells books on this topic). Second, the research we do have from neuroscience only reiterates what good educators have always known: Learning is profoundly relational and deeply connected to emotion and safety, and when you have those elements, every student has the capacity to grow and change.

Neuroplasticity

Perhaps the most important discovery of brain science in the latter half of the twentieth century, which contributed greatly to interest in the brain and education, was the understanding of the concept of neuroplasticity. Where science once "showed" that intelligence is innate and unchanging and that the brain develops during a critical period in early childhood and then becomes static, new brain science has shown that the brain can change (is plastic) well into adulthood. What is ironic is that any teacher would have said this to be true from experience until science, with its limited and incorrect research on intelligence, decided it wasn't.

Stress, Trauma, and the Brain

Another important recent discovery has been that despite the tendency of the Western scientific tradition to place the brain at the seat of rational thinking, or the mind, neuroscience has shown that the ability to think rationally requires a balanced input of emotion and feeling (Damasio 1999). In fact, it seems that cognition actually rests on an edifice of emotion and that the millions of children diagnosed as having learning-related deficits according to the *Diagnostic and Statistical Manual of Mental Disorders,* Fifth Edition (*DSM*-5) (American Psychiatric Association 2013) are actually underserved because of the way diagnostic criteria ignore the emotional seat of the brain, which is connected to our visceral state (Maté 2011; Damasio 1994; Immordino-Yang and Damasio 2007). It seems then that much of what we see diagnosed as "mental health problems" or "learning disabilities" can actually be more precisely understood not as illness but as injury or trauma (Maté 2011; Herman 1992; Burstow 2015; Frances 2013).

Buzzwords like growth mindset, social and emotional learning (SEL), and trauma-informed care (TIC) (Figure 1.2) are a part of almost every education circle now. While they are discussed today as modern holistic frameworks, it's important we recognize these are fundamental aspects of good teaching that had always been around until they were stripped away in the pursuit of "scientific" legitimacy. And now, we see these concepts co-opted into individualized interventions and branded under labels as part of new educational economies, as if they are not just essential elements of teaching that every good teacher understands. Education is full of such cases of "science" finally catching up to it. Take the aftermath of the global pandemic in 2020: researchers began publishing data showing that the stress and isolation of pandemic life led to neuroinflammation, even in those who never contracted COVID, affecting memory, attention, and cognitive processing (Brusaferri et al. 2022). Educators who already knew this are now being told to do what they always intuitively knew to do but couldn't because of the system they have to operate under. New scientific discoveries, it seems, often simply affirm lived experience, but that experience is never legitimatized unless empirically proven.

FIGURE 1.2

Growth Mindset

Coined by psychologist Carol Dweck, growth mindset is the idea that abilities and intelligence are not fixed and innate but can be developed through effort, learning, and persistence (Dweck 2008). At some point it seems, someone had to write it down: yes, humans can learn. The obviousness of this concept did not stop it from becoming a multimillion-dollar industry. But the issue is even deeper. Efforts around growth mindset and other research like it have come to show themselves as nothing more than a rebranding of old eugenic, ableist, and capitalist messaging: everything will be better if you just develop a growth mindset, everything will be better if you just learn to control your thoughts, everything will be better if you just learn to regulate your emotions, everything will be better if you just identify your childhood trauma or attachment bond, everything will be better if you just fix your gut health, and the list goes on, creating what is essentially a new "wellness" route to the white supremacy pipeline (Cederström and Spicer 2015). Once again, the burden is put solely on the individual, ignoring structural oppression, material conditions, and collective trauma. It is the same old "pull yourself up by your bootstraps" ideology, rebranded for new TED TALKS® and classroom posters, promising liberation through self-discipline and simple mind shifts, conveniently selling both the wound and the cure.

Social and Emotional Learning

Social and emotional learning (SEL) is an educational framework developed to teach students five core competencies: self-awareness, self-management, social awareness, relationship skills, and responsible decision-making. Originally intended to support students' emotional intelligence and interpersonal development, SEL is now widely implemented in schools as a way to improve academic outcomes, classroom behavior, and long-term well-being. Many abolitionist and critical educators have in fact criticized SEL for being whitewashed and actually a hidden form of new policing of racialized children (Kaler-Jones 2020; Simmons 2019) while research already shows that SEL efforts regularly leave behind children with learning disabilities (Cipriano, Horowitz, and Rappolt-Schlichtmann 2021). Once again, frameworks like SEL put the burden on the individual to learn how to better self-regulate or display resilience with little effort put into challenging the conditions that create distress. By reinforcing white, middle-class behavioral norms under the guise of care, we manage students' emotions rather than address them, all while creating contradictory dynamics for educators. While some children are over-disciplined for not regulating the "right" ways, others are excused from accountability under a blanket of stress or trauma narratives. How would this change if we recognized what we observe with children not as deficits or disorders—even when reframed as "skills to be developed" through SEL—but as expressions of political and systemic issues and as signs of being out of harmony with their natural environments and needs?

Trauma-Informed Care

Trauma-informed care (TIC) refers to an organizational framework and approach that recognizes the widespread impact of trauma and seeks to actively avoid re-traumatization. In theory, the framework seeks to address the systemic and structural roots of trauma—such as racism, poverty, and social injustice—while actively working to transform oppressive environments. Here, too, we find that although the idea of trauma-informed care is meant to foster empathy, once again, the focus is on the symptoms exhibited by the individual rather than on meaningful structural and political shifts. As a result, this framework unintentionally individualizes trauma. TIC has substantial and meaningful research and literature behind it, but in practice has become yet another inadequate solution that encourages coping strategies rather than actively working on dismantling oppressive systems.

TIC both encourages and limits educators and therapists by directing attention toward managing and containing behavior rather than addressing root causes. True trauma-informed care calls for deep systemic change first and foremost. It requires confronting the political, economic, and social forces that generate trauma and perpetuate inequity. Unfortunately, what I often see today is this phrase simply being used as a branding strategy for websites and materials that simultaneously display signs and language that are racist and ableist.

This commercialization has resulted in a dilution of the radical potential of this approach, reducing it to little more than lip service that maintains the status quo rather than challenging it.

So, it would seem that despite all our new frameworks and rhetoric, what we continue to ignore in our capitalist ideologies (despite the lessons of the pandemic) is that in a society where we are less and less connected to our feelings and to each other, it would make sense that our brains are less and less efficient in dealing with our external world, thus creating an epidemic of learning disabilities and mental health disorders, especially among already isolated and marginalized populations who suffer disconnection. But what we repeatedly ignore in all our new reforms and language is that the conditions for healthy brain development, especially for the prefrontal cortex—loving connection, attunement, environmental safety—are less and less available to children today (Lipton 2005; Maté 2000). All this goes to show that a lot more goes into what is happening in children's lives that is hindering their ability to socially interact well, to pay attention well, to learn well, and to be self-regulated than our tests can detect or our new reform programs can address. Yet we continue to use brain science to address the behavior and symptoms while the emotional edifice and structural reasons causing the child to either act out or display learning difficulties are ignored. But buzzword programs will not help students so long as we are forcing these reforms in the same old ways as we have forced other reforms instead of actually changing the material conditions of classrooms and communities. It seems we have to wait until science effectively studies the impact of capitalism on the human brain.

Is It Science or Capitalism?

More recent neuroscientific research has also shown that the mind is not separate from the body as it has historically been considered to be in Western medical and psychological models. Rather, it is a connected collective that influences and is influenced by other humans, our environment, histories, cultures, and our values and priorities and is therefore best served in the context of the relationship between the child and the guiding adult

(Damasio 2003; Maté 2011; Craig 2015; Barrett 2017; Kitayama and Uskul 2011). This means that the entire idea of searching for a "cure" is in direct contradiction to how humans work. We know that this also holds true about the therapeutic relationship. Research has shown (Norcross and Wampold 2011; Norcross and Lambert 2018; Wampold 2001) that it is the relationship itself between the therapist and the patient that is the most healing aspect of therapy, not any particular modality. And yet, just as with the proliferation of modalities like cognitive behavioral therapy (CBT) and other "evidence-based" approaches in psychology, I have watched as educators become salespeople for different programs in the private sector and administrators become salespeople for different programs under the umbrella of "reform" in the public sector. These programs then move to basically remove the educator who becomes nothing more than a delivery apparatus for the program or "the cure." And, of course, all this is done in the name of science, even as science insists that it is in human relationships that we learn most. Today, this logic is accelerating under the influence of artificial intelligence, which deepens surveillance, standardization, and dehumanization, all under the guise of personalization and efficiency.

It is therefore important for us to realize that there is a distinct line between science and business that is often blurred in our capitalist society and culture, with devastating consequences. It is disturbing to read, for example, in credible peer-reviewed scientific journals on education claims such as "every major modern business grounds itself solidly in research that is shaped by practical questions about how products function and how they can be used effectively in context" (Fischer 2009, 3) and to then see arguments like this be used to push for the "scientification" of education. As educators, we must understand that the push we sometimes feel to be more data driven, more results oriented, and more "scientific" has little to do with actual scientific research about our field and more to do with the same business-oriented view of education that has wreaked havoc in American classrooms for decades. It is disturbing, for example, to compare the expectations of the average American classroom against Tema Okun's characteristics of White Supremacy Culture (Okun n.d.). What's even more disturbing is that at the same time we set these expectations (perfectionism, either/or thinking, a sense of urgency, worship of the written word, an insistence on only one right way, etc.) we then turn and shame and criticize students for not being able to cope with these standards by telling them to do exactly the opposite of what we expect: don't be a perfectionist, think outside the box, don't be so anxious, just pay attention. The gaslighting reaches absurd levels of abuse, and as in any abusive dynamic, the victim is expected to carry the burden of their own abuse.

We must also recognize that teachers (and therapists) too are victims here. We have a very specific role to fill in this precise factory model. We are employed to help this model run. We must therefore also be regularly gaslit into following the company line—all the while being told we are in fact helping children realize the ideals of democracy and are raising independent, critical, and creative thinkers for the future. It should not surprise us to see that, despite all the discussion around evidence and data, the shift to neuroscience as the great new frontier for education is just another way to reproduce the same types of hierarchies and inequities first started with IQ testing (Pirayesh 2018), creating a kind of "neuro-phrenology" (117) in the educational landscape.

> **VOCABULARY**
>
> **Gaslighting** is a form of psychological abuse where someone manipulates another person into doubting their own sanity, memory, or reality in order to gain control over the victim, often with severe emotional and psychological effects.

There is an old adage in neuroscience: if you want to understand how something works, look at where it breaks down. We cannot "fix" our education system because we cannot manufacture love. We cannot mandate attunement. This is where we break down and, as Audre Lorde says, "the master's tools will never dismantle the Master's house" (Lorde 1984, 5). Empiricism is too narrow a tool for the expansiveness of a field like education. So as educators, we must stay skeptical and vigilant in our questioning about any Western scientific technology that aims to reform education or help us produce better brains or children. To do this, we must remember that *we* are in fact the true experts on guiding children as they grow into themselves and into their world. Just as we must remember what the true definitions and goals for education are and the important role we play as teachers in helping those goals be actualized.

GETTING CLEAR ON OUR GOALS

We stand in a time in our country today where teachers are leaving the profession in droves, tired of being devalued, micromanaged, and politicized in the worst ways. The discourse against teachers has become so hostile that there are now even proposals to replace educators with ex-miliary personnel, custodial staff, and even AI. This shows that many are ready to reduce a teacher's role to providing nothing more than discipline, maintenance, or mechanized instruction. But we are also in a time in our country where we are finally understanding the critical, essential, and important value of classroom teachers. If this was not the case, there would not be such extreme efforts to control them.

In order for teachers to step into their power, they must first become politically and critically conscious themselves. This is a concept best crystallized by the critical educator Paolo Freire (2018), who saw the development of critical consciousness—*conscientização*—as the goal of education. How can we foster *conscientização* in our students when we are not actively working to foster it in ourselves? How can we foster *conscientização* in our students when we ourselves are the products of an education that aims to constrict our consciousness in an effort to teach us to keep the line and to teach the next generation to do the same? To undo this, we must first understand the system we work in and the impact of those systems on our own thinking and teaching. The most important apprenticeship years of any teacher, it has been said, are the twelve they spend in school. American education, shaped by Western science, has always pushed for neutrality. But as we have come to understand in recent years, that push is itself the greatest political act and must be resisted. As Freire says, "There is no such thing as a *neutral* educational process. Education either functions as an instrument that is used to facilitate the integration of the younger generation into the logic of the present system and bring about conformity to it, *or* it becomes 'the practice of freedom,' the means by which men and women deal critically and creatively with reality and discover how to participate in the transformation of their world (Freire 2018, 34). Therefore, we must first begin with the dismantling of our own "education" and indoctrination so that we don't perpetuate the same systems but rather help raise the very revolutionary thinkers our system so desperately wants to suppress.

Decolonization

In their famous article "Decolonization Is Not a Metaphor," Eve Tuck and K. Wayne Yang argue the following:

> *Decolonization brings about the repatriation of Indigenous land and life; it is not a metaphor for other things we want to do to improve our societies and schools. The easy adoption of decolonizing discourse by educational advocacy and scholarship, evidenced by the increasing number of calls to "decolonize our schools," or use "decolonizing methods," or "decolonize student thinking," turns decolonization into a metaphor. As important as their goals may be, social justice, critical methodologies, or approaches that decenter settler perspectives have objectives that may be incommensurable with decolonization. Because settler colonialism is built upon an entangled triad structure of settler-native-slave, the decolonial desires of white, non-white, immigrant, postcolonial, and oppressed people, can similarly be entangled in resettlement, reoccupation, and reinhabitation that actually further settler colonialism. The metaphorization of decolonization makes possible a set of evasions, or "settler moves to innocence," that problematically attempt to reconcile settler guilt and complicity, and rescue settler futurity. (2012, 1)*

If this does not show what has happened in the years since the George Floyd murder, when the language of social justice and diversity, equity, and inclusion (DEI) entered into the public consciousness, I don't know what does. But note that this article was published in 2012—long before we had a chance to co-opt and dilute these ideas into performative gestures, rather than meaningful and transformative change.

For the record, like Tuck and Yang, I believe that true systemic decolonization can only occur through large-scale economic redistribution—a seismic shift that I do not believe can occur without the complete dismantling of the American political and economic system in its current form. So when I refer to "decolonization" here, I am not referring to decolonizing the larger system. Rather, I am speaking about the decolonization of our minds and of the ways education and culture shape us to internalize, reproduce, and uphold colonial values and structures. It remains to be seen whether we reach a critical mass, or change comes by force, or nothing changes at all. But what I do know is that we have power over one system and that is ourselves. And that is where we can begin. I cannot force you to do the required work for that growth any more than you could for your students or anyone else. It is deeply personal, and it must be chosen.

This is why I sometimes become frustrated when I am asked for "solutions" during professional development sessions or other forums where I often spend much of the time offering a critique of the status quo. The demand for "having an answer" (often accompanied by an implied, "and if you don't, then be quiet") reflects the very positivist logic I'm arguing against. Western scientific training has conditioned us to believe that all problems have clear and tidy solutions if we only think hard or long enough to find them. But transformation is not a neat, linear, or causal process. Change, both personal and social, is a complex, unpredictable, and emergent process. There is no universal blueprint or step-by-step checklist. There is no template I can copy and hand to all teachers to teach from. Solutions must be cocreated, in real time, by the local stakeholders in response to their particular context and they must reflect their histories, values, relationships, and circumstances.

Such processes require their own contextual inspiration. You would not ask an artist to tell you ahead of time exactly what they will create. If they do and they can, that is not art. The same holds here. What you might create in your classroom and in your relationships as a result of this work will and must differ from what someone else will create. What is offered here is not a blueprint. Rather, it is a set of principles and guidelines and a framework to serve as a loose container within which you have total creative license. If as an educator you find the idea of not having a step-by-step process to model disconcerting, your first task is to sit with that. The invitation here is to engage in the act and state of creativity. It is to engage in the process of better understanding and clarifying the questions, *your* questions. This shift itself can require years—if not decades or even a lifetime—of deconditioning and decolonization of our thinking.

In this book, I envision a different kind of schooling system, a working model to aim for. In fact, the work of a teacher is not to give the answers. There are no answers. Answers are emergent processes. Solutions are self-organizing, with no clear beginning or end or previous planning. Similarly, they are often not perfect as they must reflect not an ideal but what is possible in a three-dimensional world under the pressures of countless confounding variables. Our job is to help more accurately describe and situate the problem. What happens after that, in terms of the decolonization of our systems—decolonization that is not just a metaphor—you will have to create.

THE FRAMEWORK

The framework in this book is made up of four elements: collective ideology, connected experience, contextualized diagnosis, and communized care. I call this the 4C framework. In Chapter 2, I will provide a foundation for this work through building consciousness and gaining awareness through critical education. In Chapter 3, we will explore the ways in which we are connected and interrogate our standards for assessment. In Chapter 4, we will consider how disability, and our understanding of disability, is influenced by our surroundings. In Chapter 5, we will reenvision systems of support. And finally, in Chapter 6, I will introduce a new vision for a future anchored in radical love.

While we can trace back the roots of our education system to the democratic ideals of John Dewey and others, the fact is, we also see evidence of a competitive, white supremacist, positivist system aimed at raising future workers for a capitalist economy. At the same time, in the history of oppression and violence against our most vulnerable students, we also see a history of radical resistance by them. Our history shows that many of us, whether regular classroom or special education teachers or clinicians, don't realize that often our role is unfortunately to help uphold these systems of oppression and produce the workers society needs while quietly dispensing with those who don't fit. The latest push we see for the control of teachers is in response to the expansion of American consciousness that emerged after the events of the last few years and prompted the critical interrogation of our systems, including our history.

While the tensions we feel today might feel new in some ways, they have existed since the start of our union. The good news is, there have also existed blueprints of resistance put forth by critical and liberatory educators to help guide us now. This book invites you to ask, at this new, but old, juncture, fundamental questions in response to the tensions we feel: What is the purpose of education, and what is the true role of educators in our education system? More importantly, this book aims to ask a question of you: Are you, as a teacher, ready to step into your power and your role as the single most important change agent in society?

As a bicultural, bilingual, first-generation immigrant working specifically with children marginalized in an ableist education system, I want to help you find *your* answers to that question while encouraging you to see both why and how every teacher should (and often does, simply by existing) resist and push back against a system that aims to limit your role as an educator to a babysitter at worst and an evaluator at best. My hope is that you'll use the framework provided in this book, and the stories of my own work fighting for the learning rights of children with learning differences, to build more liberatory classrooms and to step into the most important (and therefore oppressed) public role in a democracy—that of an educator—with confidence and resolve.

This Work Is Hard

The issues I am asking you to engage with in this book are difficult. This is not the kind of book that aims to give simple steps for creating more inclusive classrooms or tips on how to find your calling as a teacher. Instead, the ask is for real and deep engagement with serious personal, psychological, professional, political, and even spiritual matters that impact us as both educators and human beings. When I first came across some of the ideas I'm presenting here, making the realizations I hope you'll make as you move forward, I struggled. On the one hand, I felt as if I was finally being seen, heard, and validated. On the other hand, I felt I was losing all that I had ever believed in—my hope, my faith, my vocation, even my sense of self. It's a strange tension to reside in, but as one of the major points of this book is to understand and even invite tension as a necessary condition for growth, I hope that you'll be willing to practice sitting with that tension.

This book can bring up different things for different people. Our backgrounds, positionalities (Figure 1.3) (Pollock 2021), training, education, and beliefs will greatly impact how we come to this work, what we can tolerate from it, and what we will need to put off until we are ready. Be patient with yourself. There is no finish line. The learning I am asking you to do, and in turn the learning I hope you'll invite your students to do, is infinite. It will never end, so there is no sense worrying about time. Time is meaningless in infinity. The key is to be truthful with yourself and go at the pace that feels right.

In my experience, most teachers, certainly teachers who would buy a book like this, believe in the good of the world. They are mostly themselves what we would consider, in our values of duality, good people who want to do good in the world, namely by helping to raise and guide the next generation of good people. This is not just something we believe about ourselves, but something the culture, despite how poorly it pays teachers and how harshly it treats them as of late, also believes about teaching and the work of educators. No one gets into education to hurt people. It may be jarring to hear me say that that is exactly what we are all doing.

My hope is that you will trust me long enough, as you read the ideas in this book, to allow me to break down the American education system and show you its roots, its beginnings, and why they in no way match our highest ideals and to reveal to you a system intently built on imprisoning the human mind and even killing the human spirit. I hope you will then trust me to also break down your positive identity as a teacher, as a healer, and as a guide in order to show you that such assumptions, when based on faulty beginnings, simply cannot be true.

Positionality is

1. the social and political context that creates your identity, and
2. how your identity influences and biases your perception of and outlook on the world.

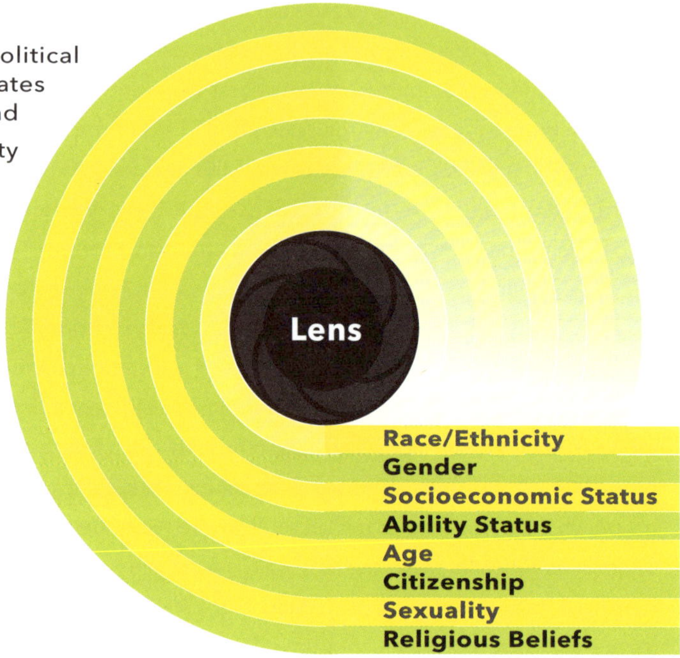

FIGURE 1.3

This is the work of decolonization. It begins with the careful, surgical process of opening up our own psyches as well as the psyche of our culture, our government, and our institutions in order to examine and interrogate them. A big part of colonization is having one hegemonic way of thinking become everyone's way of thinking in order to exert control. Colonization is not limited to the forceful taking of land, language, and culture in order to impose our own way of thinking. Colonization can happen in the essential space between a parent and a child, a teacher and a student. Those of us charged with the important task of helping a child build a consciousness, a sense of self, a way of thinking and seeing the world, can easily force our own thinking on them, sometimes absolutely, often unconsciously. In turn, in an attempt to survive, the child often forgoes their own potential consciousness and instead takes on the parents' or teachers' thinking, forming a new consciousness that helps push forward the same agenda.

The same cycle exists in the world of teaching and education, where teachers play the role of child and the education system is like a narcissistic parent or dogmatic teacher who tells us they care about us, want to support us to support others, but is all the while betraying us behind the scenes to push their own agenda. Like an innocent child, we as teachers believe in the love and high ideals the system sells us, create ourselves in its image, and then without realizing it become an instrument of its hegemony.

This can be a hard pill to swallow, to recognize ourselves as one of the "bad guys." But until we do that interrogation, we cannot sever the old conditionings and come out the other side ready to build a new and free consciousness, one that reflects our own ideals and not the hidden agendas and curriculums of our conditioning.

I know this to be true because I have done it, now countless times. When I first started working in Los Angeles, the private schools many of my clients attended would not even consider the idea of a learning difference. After a decade of advocacy by me and others like me, almost every school today has a "learning specialist" on staff, some even asking me and others like me to come in to train their teachers on learning disabilities. Does this mean that these schools have suddenly changed their ways and embraced inclusion? No. We don't even have that in the public school system despite decades of disability laws in place. But for my students, getting some acknowledgment of their challenges along with some accommodations, however small, is a big improvement.

This kind of small, glacially paced response to ongoing advocacy and resistance is difficult for someone like me to accept. The frustration of one step forward, two steps back, of year in and year out just to make the same points, takes a toll. But when I see that this is exactly what my students do, that their struggle to function in an ableist world will be the work of a lifetime, of many lifetimes, my resolve is renewed. Similarly, when I look at the history of revolution and resistance, of peoples fighting for decades, sometimes centuries, and for the ongoing everlasting fight of life itself, I am reminded again that time is not a factor in eternity and that life is not made for the impatient. If you are not ready and willing to see and to embrace the big wins in your small fights, this is not the profession for you. Teaching, like therapy, is ultimately about self-healing and about holding space for the healing of others. But healing and learning, decolonizing and building anew, is never linear. In large part, the role of those of us in "guidance" professions is to teach that the steps back are just as relevant and just as important as the steps forward. There will never be a time when we are done. To become a guide for others, we must first ourselves work to be fully capable of experiencing life, which is anything but linear, anything but only good, and anything but done. We are constantly healing, hurting, growing, becoming, and unbecoming. There is no arrival. There is no "done."

It may seem sad to draw upon Victor Frankl (1946) here, as if to equate teaching in an American school today to surviving a Nazi concentration camp, but the fact is, Frankl's point applies: no matter the circumstances, a freedom of choice exists within us all. If ignorance is bliss, then knowledge and enlightenment is the embrace of suffering and grief. This is not a concept that sits well in a culture obsessed with success and happiness and instant gratification. But as anyone who has spent one day teaching in a classroom can attest, if you are not ready to suffer and to grieve, you have no business in the world of teaching and learning.

My point here is not to say that we must accept our low status and our oppression and our suffering, but rather that if we want to use it to break free and to teach our students to do the same, we have to be willing to feel pain. This is what it means to be a revolutionary. This is what it means to do the work of being and becoming a conscious human being.

A Pedagogy of Hope

There is a famous interview recording with the late Palestinian author, scholar, and resistance leader Ghassan Kanafani. Around the time the Black Lives Matter protests were at their height, a video of this interview was making the rounds on social media (Kanafani 1970). In it, the interviewer, an Australian reporter, encourages him to engage in peace talks. "Why don't you talk?" he asks, to which a confused Kanafani asks to whom and for what. Talk to "stop the death, and the misery," the reporter continues, "the destruction, the pain," because better to be alive in such circumstances than dead. To this Kanafani replies, "Maybe to you, but to us, to liberate our country, to have dignity, to have respect, to have our mere human rights, is something as essential as life itself." It is a powerful exchange in which we get a glimpse of what a true revolutionary spirit looks and feels like, just as we get a glimpse of the gaslighting of the status quo that pushes us to use language like "conflict" or "civil war" instead of "liberation movement." Kanafani pushes back.

Kanafani was later murdered by the Mossad when he and his seventeen-year-old niece were blown up in a car bomb, leaving behind only his poems, novels, and other writings, as well as the video of this interview. Meanwhile, since his passing decades ago, the plight of the Palestinian people has not changed. In the comments of this interview I was surprised to find such hopelessness, with many young people making comments along the lines of "and fifty years later, nothing has changed." I felt moved to respond to one such comment and I wrote simply: "I used to think this too. But fifty years later, Palestine is still resisting and if that's not the very definition of hope, I don't know what is."

I was shocked by the response to this comment. So many people seemed desperate for this reframing. I had so many thank-yous and comments like "you just changed my whole outlook" and "I think I believe in life again." This is an extremely important issue in social justice and healing work. This kind of work often feels thankless and pointless, as if we are not getting anywhere. But the point is the resistance. Fifty years later, Kanafani's words are still fueling and supporting a resistance movement halfway across the world and halfway across the century. That is success. When Angela Davis (2016) and other Black revolutionary leaders who have long seen the connection between Palestinian and Black struggles say that "freedom is a constant struggle," we need to understand that at the core of that phrase is hope, not hopelessness.

It has been incredibly difficult to feel hopeful in the past few years. The ongoing collective trauma of the pandemic, wealth inequality, climate crisis, the rise of fascism, a war in Europe, a genocide in the Middle East, the rise of new technologies . . . the list continues . . . has made it so our collective mental health is hanging on by a thread. But this is exactly when we need to develop a "pedagogy of hope" and to understand that we are not just passively receiving the unbearable weight of all this. We *are* in fact in a state of active and collective resistance and all our exhaustion and dread is actually quite meaningful and, dare I say, proof of hope.

By simply existing, by feeling earnestly the pain of injustice, we are in fact naming it as such, and that is resistance. This is why today I would stay with my student Andrew. I would work to teach him the value of his resistance, whatever path he takes. And I would help support him in that resistance. When Audre Lorde (2017) speaks of "self-care"—a term that has been bastardized by capitalism and the invention of the self-care industry—she is referring to the importance of fueling ourselves as we withstand, absorb, and process the pain of the unnecessary injustices created by values that place greed over love and of reframing that work as active resistance for the very reclaiming of our humanity. As teachers we not only need to do this for ourselves; we need to help our students do the same. The Palestinian people may never see justice, but they will also never know the true hopelessness of accepting injustice and assimilating into its oblivion and darkness. We may not be able to save our planet or our species even (though I believe we can) but we can be sure that we safeguard our humanity. The proof is in the pain and the grief we feel. "Horse runs, bird flies, human feels," goes the proverb. Often to be a "keeper of hope," as Kanafani understood, is to have the willingness to feel through the darkness and remember that life without our humanity is no life at all.

I say this not to convince you that teaching is a hopeless act or that our job is to be martyrs. Rather, my hope is to help prime you for the pain that is to come, the pain that is inevitable in any growth, with less concern for where the growth may lead—none of us know that right now—but a willingness to see that growth itself is the goal. And yes, our efforts may, they just may, lead somewhere worthwhile, but the most worthy result of your efforts will be the change you see in yourself.

CHAPTER 2

COLLECTIVE IDEOLOGY

The first time I sat with Elijah for an educational therapy session, I was blown away by his intelligence. We met at his school library, even though getting the space had been contentious, as his school principal was not supportive of me being brought in to help Elijah. His small but very wealthy school was just a few short blocks from the beach in Santa Monica, and as we sat across from each other on tiny birchwood chairs, Elijah's blue eyes glistening under the sun pouring through the window, the ocean breeze and seagull calls surrounding us in the glass-walled library, all I could think was, "I wish every child went to a school like this."

Except school was not exactly working for Elijah. At eight years old and in the second grade, he had tried for three years to learn how to read at this small progressive school his parents had handpicked for him because of its philosophy of meeting the needs of *all* kids, a phrase I had seen repeated throughout their impressively produced website. But Elijah could barely write or even recognize all the letters of the alphabet.

Elijah's parents had shared their concerns with his teachers and school administrators on several occasions but had repeatedly been told not to worry, that every child learns at their own pace, and that they shouldn't push Elijah. Elijah had therefore come to me with no previous testing or any recommendations from his school. His mother had finally decided to listen to her own instincts and ignore the nearly three years of advice from the educators in his life. As a result, the school principal, upset by my recommendation for testing, had questioned the parents' decision to have me work with him at school.

It did not take long, or much educational testing (though that came later), for me to see that Elijah displayed many of the classic signs of dyslexia: difficulty with sound processing, guessing words when reading, misreading function words, etc. When my screening revealed the severity of the problem, a complete inability to blend and pull apart sounds, I referred him for more thorough evaluation to a psychologist—a recommendation that immediately prompted his principal, Billy, to question my expertise. Billy was a jovial man in his sixties who had established the school about three decades prior in response to his own frustrations with the education system. Although he had a doctorate, he insisted I simply call him by his first name because "everyone here is equal." I can't deny that when I first walked the grounds of his building, which had started out as a small neighborhood school but had grown into "a multimillion-dollar nonprofit" as he proudly described it, I was struck by the quaint feel, the colorful walls, the thoughtful gardens and playgrounds, and the big classrooms occupied by no more than twelve students per class. Every classroom we walked into looked engaged in—some students reading, some doing science experiments, some cooking. "We expose children to everything and let them pick for themselves, but that doesn't mean that we don't have rigor," Billy told me as he took me from class to class. "Our kids do amazing things—some are reading classics, some are building complex robots and doing high-level math, but we let them lead, we let them discover what they love and support what they gravitate toward."

Everything Billy was saying sounded right, but as he led me from one beautiful corner of his school to the next, something felt off. Walking up the stairs to the roof garden, I saw, in brightly colored letters on a mural of flowers, houses, and animals that the kids had clearly painted, the famous quote often attributed to Albert Einstein: "Everybody is a genius, but if you judge a fish by its ability to climb a tree, it will live its whole life believing that it is stupid."

Back in his office, a big, bright room with thoughtfully framed children's drawings all over the walls and a large window with a view of the Pacific, Billy felt it was time to explain to me why he didn't feel Elijah needed testing or educational therapy or any other "push" to "force" him to read. "I've been doing this for thirty years," he said. "Kids do better when left to their own devices, without us forcing our tests and labels on them."

In addition to the paintings and quotes on the walls, I had noticed a few other things on our tour, like the fact that outside of one Black teacher and one Indian student, I was the only person of color on that campus. Also, I knew that Billy had never actually taught in a classroom himself, that his school cost thirty thousand dollars a year to attend, and that the majority of the kids he enrolled came from families where their education, if they decided they wanted one, would be secured because of their parents' privileges. Billy's school was a feeder school to the top middle and (later) high schools in Los Angeles, and I knew, because I had some of Billy's former students in some of those schools who struggled, that kids could get accepted even if they didn't score highly on their tests so long as Billy put in a call. I also knew they would continue to move forward because their parents could continue to provide them supports like me. Because of all this, I wasn't sure I could trust Billy's anecdotal experience or his educational philosophy. It seemed so disconnected from the realities of my own experiences.

Elijah also came from a privileged family. If he never learned to read in elementary school, he would likely still be okay. He would likely still be okay even if he never graduated from high school. Not all this was because of his privilege. That first day, when I sat across from him at the library and watched as he struggled to make even basic vowel sounds, I could already see why Billy and Elijah's teachers might think he would eventually figure it out. He was incredibly articulate, sharing his thoughts about everything from weather and wind currents (I had mentioned how surprisingly warm it was for a fall day) to the latest book his parents were reading to him (Tolkien). But as we know, that's not how a learning disability works.

I had not gone in that day to convince Billy that he was wrong about Elijah, that Elijah did in fact have a learning disability, or that denying disability and covering aspects of reality he wasn't comfortable with under layers of colorful paint and fancy quotes wasn't just ableist, it was a huge disservice to the children he was trying to serve. I had simply gone in to make the case that Elijah required a different approach to reading, and if his school truly "met children where they are" as their marketing material suggested, Billy had a responsibility to bring in a different approach to reading to help Elijah and others like him. And I told him that—not in exactly those words, but as best as I could without injuring his false utopia too much. "It's true that we can't measure kids using the same criteria," I told him, "and I think there is absolutely a case to be made about dyslexic brains not being disabled but actually differently wired for important variability purposes." I continued, hoping to help him see I didn't take a deficit view, "But the fact is we live in a world where you have to be able to read in order to function. That may not hold true fifty years from now, but right now, we have to make sure Elijah and other kids like him learn to read."

Billy didn't look happy. "I don't believe in hours of 'kill and drill' therapies that torture kids," I tried to reassure him, "but Elijah needs a different approach. He will struggle with the whole-language approach because his brain is wired differently. If we assume all kids will figure it out in their own time, isn't that just another one-size-fits-all approach? Isn't it our job to figure out what *he* needs and adjust accordingly?"

Billy looked confused. He couldn't comprehend that in his desire to create perfection he had actually created a somewhat oppressive environment in which the real needs of some kids were being denied in the name of freedom and child-centeredness. This is what happens when we don't understand things at an ontological level. We rebrand white supremacist capitalist patriarchal thinking in progressive slogans and pretty colors and think we are promoting social justice.

IDEOLOGIES AND ONTOLOGIES

To truly understand our teaching—and transform it—we have to look beneath the surface. As educators, we don't usually think in terms of philosophical foundations like ontology, epistemology, methodology, and methods (see Figure 2.1). (For a more comprehensive explanation of these philosophical concepts, see Michael Crotty [1998] or Katie Moon and Deborah Blackman [2014; 2017].) These concepts often live in research theory or academic philosophy. But they shape everything we do. Our classroom practices don't

Ontology → Epistemology → Methodology → Methods

	Definition	**In Teaching**
Ontology	• **The study of being.** Concerns the nature of reality and what exists. • It asks: *What exists? What is the nature of reality?* • Foundation level–shapes epistemology	***What do you believe is real?*** This is your worldview. It shapes what you believe exists, what matters, and what is possible in the world. Ontology is the study of being.
Epistemology	• **The study of knowledge.** Concerns how knowledge is created, what counts as valid knowledge, and how we come to know it. • It asks: *What is knowledge? How do we know what we know?* • Informed by ontology, shapes methodology	***What do you believe counts as knowledge?*** This is about how you think knowledge is created, who holds it, and whose voices are valid.
Methodology	• **The overall approach or philosophy of how we engage with knowledge and learning and rationalize the choice and use of particular methods in a field of study.** • It asks: *How do we approach gaining knowledge about the world? What underpins our approach?* • Guided by epistemology, informs methods	***What is your overall approach to teaching and learning?*** This is your philosophy of education in action–how you structure learning, whose needs are centered, and what you believe learning should do.
Methods	• **The specific techniques and procedures used to collect and analyze data.** These are the tools or instruments used in research or inquiry. • Chosen based on methodology	***What strategies and tools do you use?*** These are your day-to-day practices–the specific strategies, tools, or practices used to enact knowledge construction. (How do you plan lessons, teach, assess, manage the classroom, or intervene?)

FIGURE 2.1

exist in a vacuum. They grow from deep-rooted beliefs about what is real, what counts as knowledge, how learning should happen, and what is worth teaching. If we want to decolonize education, we have to begin at the roots.

In American education, we have long operated under the cultural belief that curriculum and policy, and education as a field, is objective, apolitical, merit-based, and neutral. In recent years, with the introduction of tools like critical race theory and cultural shifts like the racial uprisings of 2020 and the pandemic's exposure of systemic inequities, more educators and scholars began to name how ideology shapes everything from policy to curriculum design. This shift then sparked a new backlash, with movements pushing to ban "divisive" and "un-American" concepts, all to reveal that education is in fact and has always been deeply ideologically fueled. I want to invite you in this book to sit with this tension—not the tension between which ideology is best or most correct, but with the deeper tension of recognizing that it is in fact part of our job and our ethical responsibility as educators to understand, trace, and unpack the ideologies at the core of our field and to examine the ways in which they shape our beliefs about education and its practice.

Our ideologies begin at the ontological level, the most fundamental level at which we consider the very existence of reality and ask what the very nature of existence is. In other words, in Western ontologies, we tend to ask, "What is the nature of being?" and right at this level we diverge from ontologies that ask, "What is the nature of becoming?", as nothing is. Without diving too deeply into the philosophical differences between Western philosophers like Aristotle and Descartes and non-Western philosophers that do not separate the human from nature and the mind from the body, it is important to note that, ontologically speaking, Western thinking has always been structured around a fragmented and hierarchical worldview. Such a view assumes that everything can be traced back to singular, linear causes, leading to frameworks that can then easily justify and normalize a reality that is not only disconnected but also racist, sexist, and ableist. The moment we see ourselves as outside reality and able to deconstruct and study it as opposed to cocreating reality as a part of all that exists, we assume a kind of godlike position (Harding 1986). This viewpoint leads to what bell hooks refers to as white supremacist capitalist patriarchy (WSCP) (hooks 1984, 51;

hooks 2000b, 46), an ideological positioning that would naturally grow out of positivist Western ontological thinking—the idea that all knowledge must be based on observable, empirical evidence and logical reasoning. When I assume that I stand outside reality and have the capacity to define it, I must start with the assumption that I (in this case a white, heterosexual, able-bodied, neurotypical man) assume the position of "the perfect human." From there it's easy to see how a whole reality flows in which I get to reign supreme with an absolute right to exploit all that is around me. While we may not think of this mindset as present in our classrooms, it very much is. Our entire schooling system is based on IQ systems that ultimately assume a supreme cognitive ability (part of white supremacy) while ranking the world so that a particular class rules at the top and everyone else is trained to limit their capacities as human beings in order to serve that ruling class in an orderly, conformist fashion (both capitalist and patriarchal). To undo this, we must begin to question things at the ontological level.

White Supremacist Capitalist Patriarchy

If ontology and ideology are interconnected, and our ideology is fueled by, or even is, WSCP, we need to understand that concept better. What is important about this phrase is that it captures the sociological, economic, and relational aspects of existing as a human being. It is through all these lenses that we must consider our culture, and when we do, we often arrive back at hooks' phrase. It captures our culture and the ideology at its root.

This phrase, which in my opinion perfectly describes how our ontology manifests in reality, including the classroom reality, also shows that at any moment in time we are all impacted by a series of interlocking or intersectional forces. Race, gender, economics—all function simultaneously in our lives. To really understand ourselves or our students, we have to consider these interconnected prisms that encapsulate the forces that make us think, feel, and behave the way we do. Note that hooks insists on using the term *white supremacy* over *racism*, for example, in order to bring attention to the way in which the construct of whiteness shapes systems and to include the history of colonization and decolonization as well as colorism and internalized racism among people of color.

I add all this because in the classroom reality, the distinction is important. For example, as an Iranian girl growing up in a society where everyone I saw around me looked like I looked, spoke the same language I spoke, and with a few exceptions, practiced the same religion I practiced (Iran is one of the most ethnically diverse nations in the world, but from the perspective of hooks' framework of power, it can feel culturally homogenous), I was in no way exempt from the forces of WSCP shaping my reality in Iran. While some might argue that patriarchy is far more extreme in a country like Iran than anywhere in the West today, you might be surprised that I disagree. As someone who considers my childhood under the Iranian regime as a kind of upbringing in a patriarchal cult, how could I think patriarchy to be a bigger issue in a country like the United States, where women are free to dress as they like, to have (mostly) equal rights, and where feminism has been a force for decades? The answer is simple: power.

On the global scale, your average Iranian man, including the Supreme Leader of Iran himself, is keenly aware of the fact that he holds far less power than any white American man. Similarly, growing up in Iran, despite its strong stance against Westernization, each one of us was keenly aware of the power differential between us and someone who spoke English or carried an American or other Western passport. Ironically, being categorized as "white" once I arrived in the US in no way changed the material reality of my brownness up to that point or after. I bring this up because I see everywhere today a shallow discussion of issues around our intersecting identities and fights over simple binaries like Black and white, including in educational and academic settings and especially in ones that try to push forward DEI initiatives. While I do not agree with the now recent push to disassemble DEI because it discriminates against whiteness, I do think valid critiques of DEI exist. The ability for many of these programs to be rolled out in ways that do not truly interrogate white supremacist ideology at an ontological level but instead serve as a kind of rebranding of the same old hierarchies must be addressed. White supremacist capitalist patriarchy, like all the language around issues of social justice, asks that we examine relationships of power, both among ourselves and within ourselves. As Eve Tuck and K. Wayne Yang argue, the efforts to decolonize our schools have in fact become a metaphor because we are not doing the actual work of examining power relations

(Tuck and Yang 2012). But what happens if we begin to shift away from western positivist ontologies and white supremacist capitalist patriarchal ideologies toward a collective ideology?

Anyone who has ever navigated an intimate relationship knows how intricate, tangled, often subdued, but always powerful these relations are. At the core of positive intimate relationships is love. To me, love is the absence of a power differential. As I am asking you to teach from and for love, it is critical that we contextualize, examine, and understand these intricate relations of power created by our histories, by societal norms, and our positionalities. This is a primary task for you as you read the stories in this book and later as you examine your own and your students' stories.

COLLECTIVE IDEOLOGY

Collective ideology does not mean a one-size-fits-all approach for everyone, it does not mean we don't see color, it does not mean love is love. A collective ideology requires the very nuanced discernment of the differences between us and the willingness to see and acknowledge them without judgment. Billy's vision, though appealing at first glance, was actually fueled by shame, shame that he felt and carried about disability and ironically the very idea of difference itself, which was then projected onto Elijah, ultimately disabling him further.

Elijah was incredibly smart. Like many kids who struggle with the linear two-dimensional world of the written word, he had an amazing ability to think and perceive things in ways someone like me never could. He was a gifted artist and musician, an avid surfer, with the ability to move and naturally balance his small frame on skateboards and surfboards in ways I never could at his age. There is much debate, even today, about the language we use to describe difference. And while language is important, it wasn't just in the naming of Elijah's difference as a "disability" that Billy struggled. He struggled to accept that sometimes fish could struggle to swim, and that was okay.

I do not bring up Elijah's other gifts and abilities to make a case for him being of value because of his intelligence. That is just a fuller picture of the kid he was. None of us draw our value from our intelligence or what we can do, which is why there is no value lost in what we can't do. Billy's insistence that all kids are capable seemed to me like it had its roots in a great fear, a great doubt, that a kid's value, that any human or living being's value, lies in nothing more than their being. To be alive, life itself, is what gives us our value, and when we recognize that and can accept that the nature of our being is love, that being itself is consciousness, the very concept of value or the fear of the lack of it ceases to be. What is nature? What is being? The questions themselves cease. Ontology then becomes not thinking about nature but being nature. I am not outside life thinking about it and categorizing it. I am life and life is me. Asking about my value is no different than asking about the value of life itself.

It may not seem that these philosophical questions connect to our everyday issues like how we teach reading, but they do. In recent years, there has been much discussion around neurodiversity and the importance of valuing differences. But as at Elijah's school, these discussions are still steeped in WSCP ideologies. A good way to know whether we are truly decolonizing our ideologies or simply rebranding them is to check in with how we feel. Think about one of your students. What feelings come up when you are faced with the indisputable fact that that child can't do something you consider an important skill? Do you assume they feel shame, projecting your own feelings onto the child? Are you anxious to prove they are valuable despite their inability? Are you eager to insist they are fine? What if they are not fine? What if they never learn to do that thing? What comes up then? Grief? Guilt? Sadness? These feelings can help us better understand our ontological positioning and our ideology. The goal of decolonizing our ideology is to be able to see and honor the whole value of a child exactly as they are.

In Elijah's case, he did learn to read, within a year, through intensive therapy. In fact, his progress was so dramatic that the neuropsychologist who had tested him called me personally at the end of the year to say, "He no longer qualifies for the diagnosis. You fixed his dyslexia." Except I hadn't fixed it. Elijah would always be dyslexic. Yes, he had created new neuronal pathways that had helped him process sounds better. He had learned sound-to-letter correspondences and had mastered many strategies to help him in his reading. He had broken the code, but his brain would always be a dyslexic brain, and there is nothing wrong with that. My intention was never to fix it. To do so would imply I felt something was broken. Instead, I recognized that acquiring a set of skills would help Elijah navigate society more easily. This is a very tricky concept that applies to every kind of difference among humans. Specifically in education, there is a big question around whether it is our job to accept kids as they are or to shape them into what's needed for functionality and, that dreaded word, success. Sometimes the answer is A, sometimes it's B. It depends on the student. Even for the same student it can change from circumstance to circumstance. There is no universal answer around even the philosophical basis from which we approach education.

DECOLONIZING YOUR IDEOLOGY

I share Elijah's story here to show that WSCP is our pervasive ideological and ontological position. Elijah's school would probably be considered one of the most progressive schools in the country. Not only in terms of their approach to learning, but even politically, they would fall as far left as we are allowed to go in this country. At the time, for example, so much of their curriculum in elementary school was around the election of Barack Obama and the importance of acknowledging racism (the fact that the school now costs fifty thousand dollars a year to attend and that we continuously leave out issues of class and economics in our progressive discourse around change is related to WSCP, but not something I'll address here). I know because of other students I have there today that much of the curriculum has now turned toward discussing issues around gender and that many parents embrace it (some even refuse to allow their young children to identify with a gender in order to embrace the cultural discourse around fluidity). I say this to emphasize that there is no left or right in WSCP. You can have guest speakers at your school like Tiffany Jewell and Traci Baxley (and even Ibram X. Kendi) and have them run students through an antiracism workshop and educate parents on social justice parenting, as they do, and still be so deeply steeped in WSCP that you set up a school completely ignorant of its own ableist structures. While it has been said that racism is not the shark in the water, but the water itself (Myhre 2017), I would argue that WSCP gets at the issue of us not realizing we are even fish in water. The first step toward change has to be the acknowledgment of our basic existence, our formation, our culture and environment, and the acceptance that none of us, not one single person in this country, one could argue on the majority of this planet, has not been shaped, influenced, and even made in the image of WSCP. Your politics, your religion, your language, the color of your skin, other ontologies and cultures that have shaped you—none of that makes you fully immune. WSCP has been and is the pervasive global culture because of the reach, standing, and hegemony of the West. We are all fish in the same water.

Imagine swimming in the ocean all your life, your body being shaped by the water, your defenses evolving for that environment, your food coming from it, and then beginning to separate yourself from the water, one molecule at a time, while still having to exist in the ocean. It's a limited metaphor, but the point is we cannot escape our reality as fish in water. All we can do is build awareness of it. This is the first step of decolonizing work. The fish doesn't decolonize the water but rather itself through building awareness of its own existence in the water. It is the active, ongoing work of undoing your formation and indoctrination.

Two things can help us in this effort. First, acknowledging that WSCP exists in your thinking requires a certain level of humility. Second, try pinpointing power relations. Ask yourself where you are assuming hierarchy in a situation and how you might challenge it. Nonviolent communication is a framework developed by Marshall Rosenberg (2003) to help us better understand our emotions as internal signals. At its core, it teaches something simple yet powerful: our feelings arise from either unmet or met needs. Emotions like sadness, guilt, or fear point to unmet needs and tend to motivate us to take action (see Figure 2.2 for a list of feelings that can be used to guide nonviolent communication). In contrast, emotions like calm, ease, or contentment tell us that our needs are being met and we are in a more balanced, natural state. This framework isn't revolutionary or abstract. It reflects what we teach children in kindergarten when we ask them to name

SOME BASIC FEELINGS WE ALL HAVE

Feelings when needs are fulfilled			
Amazed	Fulfilled	Joyous	Stimulated
Comfortable	Glad	Moved	Surprised
Confident	Hopeful	Optimistic	Thankful
Eager	Inspired	Proud	Touched
Energetic	Intrigued	Relieved	Trustful

Feelings when needs are not fulfilled			
Angry	Discouraged	Hopeless	Overwhelmed
Annoyed	Distressed	Impatient	Puzzled
Concerned	Embarrassed	Irritated	Reluctant
Confused	Frustrated	Lonely	Sad
Disappointed	Helpless	Nervous	Uncomfortable

FIGURE 2.2

their feelings, what Western psychology affirms about emotional regulation, and what many wisdom traditions have long known. But WSCP upends this. It tells us that our unmet needs might come from a belief of assumed power or a desire to claim "rightful" power. Power assumes and requires hierarchy. So we have to ask ourselves honestly: Does the need we have stem from a hierarchical belief? Is this need arising because I believe I am supposed to have more power here, or because I am trying to claim power that has been denied me? Since power assumes hierarchy, we need to reflect to uncover whether our emotions are connected to deeper dynamics of control and domination.

Sylvia Duckworth's (2020) Wheel of Power/Privilege (Figure 2.3) is a great visual tool to help us in this reflection as it invites us to unpack where we hold privilege and where we don't. In any situation, try to pinpoint the power tensions by checking in with your feelings and asking yourself, "What if I made this vertical power dynamic horizontal? How would that shift how I feel?" And check in again.

WHEEL OF POWER/PRIVILEGE

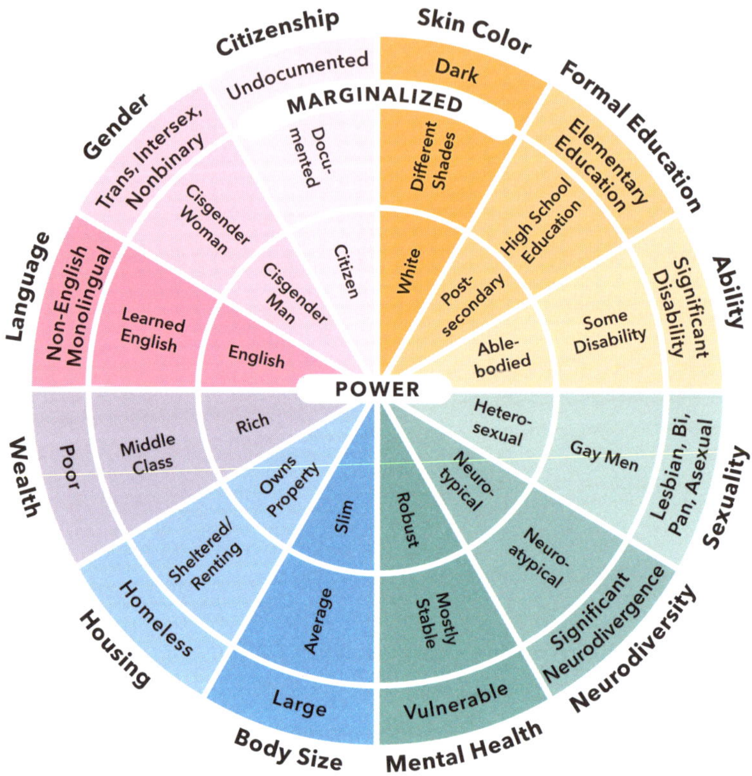

FIGURE 2.3

FROM INDIVIDUALISM TO COLLECTIVISM

As we decolonize our ontologies, we don't move toward a more collective ontology and ideology—they are what naturally emerge. As we gain awareness of ourselves and the world, we begin to see, to feel even, the oneness that is so intentionally and expertly severed by WSCP. A toppling over happens as our world view shifts from vertical hierarchies, categories, and laws toward horizontal, itinerant, and more ethical standings. This is not something we aim for—this is the true nature of things, and it is revealed when we put down the tools of empiricism that have gaslit us into believing in a distorted view of nature.

Our current ideology with its roots in Christianity and capitalism teaches us that individuals are solely responsible for themselves. In fact, the United States consistently ranks among the highest (if not *the* highest) (World Population Review 2025) on Geert Hofstede's Individualism Index (Hofstede et al. 2010). A high score means the society has lower social frameworks and individuals are expected to look after themselves. In the United States, it is generally believed that those with grit, intelligence, and the willingness to work hard are the ones who will "pull themselves up by their bootstraps." It is not uncommon to refer to our society as a "meritocracy" despite evidence to the contrary (Mark 2020). Our entire educational and special education system is based around this view to the extent that even when we build a school like Elijah's, the goal is to provide time and opportunity for everyone's genius to come through and for everyone to "succeed."

This is ultimately a misinterpretation of Darwinian evolution and the survival-of-the fittest concept that was actually coined and pushed into the culture by eugenicists (Spencer 1864; Kevles 1995; Gould 1981). (Herbert Spencer, who promoted measuring intelligence in primitive races, moved to create "racial psychology" in the late 1890s.) This view is in direct contrast to how nature actually works and how civilizations have evolved. The famous anthropologist Margaret Mead is often cited as saying that the first sign of civilization in an ancient culture is a femur (thigh bone) that had been broken and then healed. A broken femur that has healed is evidence that someone stayed with the injured person, bound the wound, carried them to safety, and tended them through recovery, standing in stark contrast to what happens in so-called civilizations based on the survival of the fittest (Dettwyler 1991; Konner 2010).

Whether you accept a mended femur bone as a sign of civilization or not, the fact is that history shows that the advancement of human civilization results from us working together, not competing. Despite our culture's myths about superheroes, no one person alone has ever created change, yet our school systems are set up to find and reward these mythical superheroes. Even our stories about educators themselves fall into this category. We have ample books and films about the one "hero teacher" who comes to save and fix and inspire students oppressed by systemic issues they never even acknowledge in the story. Nowadays we hear about how our disabilities are actually our "superpowers," again showing our obsession with competition and success.

A collective ideology, in contrast, emphasizes the importance and value of every person. It is the opposite of an individualist perspective in which everyone is independently competing in a zero-sum game and responsible for only themselves and perhaps their immediate family or small in-group. In collectivist thinking, each individual is believed to be an inherently valuable member of society, and from birth their success is strongly tied to the success of the larger group, humanity. In the most idealistic version of collectivism, the existence of power over another has been eradicated.

Once we've begun to work toward decolonizing our own thinking and undoing our own schooling, we can allow more valid science, research, and learning to occur in our classrooms. Would our students aim to compete with each other, would they marginalize and bully those who are different if left to their own devices, without our indoctrination? I ask my students this every time we come to reading William Golding's *Lord of the Flies*, which continues to be required reading across schools public and private. As critics of the book have pointed out, what Golding describes as human nature is one white man's view. And yet year after year, decade after decade, we traumatize children by presenting the horrors of that book to them as human nature. What we see in reality is actually quite different, however. When I look at communities who have been struck by environmental catastrophes, for example, including my own, I mostly see people helping each other.

Hidden Curriculums

As we decolonize our own thinking, what also emerges is our hidden curriculums. As Apple (1990), Fromm (1956), and many others posit, a hidden curriculum exists in all societies: our ideological values are communicated to us, taught to us, without our knowledge. Behind every school curriculum, there is a kind of Orwellian reality that is both naturalized and normalized as common sense and embedded into education (Darder 2012). The hidden curriculum then consists of "the norms and values that are implicitly, but effectively, taught in schools and that are not usually talked about" (Apple 1990, 84). Some examples include the great psychological premises of American education: (a) that the aim of life is happiness, that is, maximum pleasure, and (b) that egotism, selfishness, and greed (which the system needs to generate in order to function) actually lead to harmony and peace (Fromm 1976).

This has been occurring to a large extent as the collective consciousness has been decolonizing, leading to culture wars over what is taught in the classrooms. As Giroux (1981) argues:

> *The hidden curriculum represents one of the most important conceptual tools by which radicals can explore the dialectical relationships and tensions that accompany the process of reproduction at the level of day-to-day classroom interactions. . . . To make sense of the hidden curriculum means that schools have to be analyzed as agents of legitimization, organized to produce and reproduce the dominant categories, values, and social relationships necessary for the maintenance of the larger society.* (72)

It is imperative for us to realize that the fights occurring at school board meetings today are a fight for the very existence of the ontological and ideological makings of this country. To try to make sense of the hidden curriculums in our practice we have to acknowledge that our practices are legitimating agents that work to produce and reproduce the dominant values and social relationships necessary for the maintenance of the status quo (Paraskeva 2011). Decolonizing them means that we are dismantling the status quo. This is why I believe it has never been more important to be a teacher in America than now and why there is no more significant job in the country today.

It is the teacher's job to dig, to question, to decolonize, and to guide their students to do the same as layer after layer of these hidden curriculums are peeled away until what is left is the true curriculum of life: love.

SELF-ASSESSMENT

I was once asked to lead a social justice group for an organization of which I am a member. Following the George Floyd murder, I had asked in a leadership meeting why the organization had not issued a statement. This request led, as it often does, to having the only nonwhite member of the group doing the DEI work for free. I accepted to help push for much-needed change in the organization so that my own work with them would feel less uncomfortable. But what I soon came to discover was that all the liberal white women who had enthusiastically joined the group didn't seem to realize that it was they who had to do the bulk of the decolonizing antiracism work, not me.

I soon left the group. In truth, though, I felt pushed out because it seemed that what the group wanted to do was just replicate the same white-savior charity mindset where they "studied," for example, the school-to-prison pipeline and raised money for interventions and rebranded them as DEI without taking a deeper look at themselves and their own role. With all the research coming out showing that DEI efforts do not work (Zheng 2024; Wang et al. 2024), we should not be surprised that these efforts actually damage true social justice efforts by watering down the work and engulfing it into the WSCP framework.

As I told the social justice group members who pushed back hard against my suggestions, the work of DEI is with the colonizer. It is not enough to ask a disabled student, for example, to lead the class in a lesson on what it feels like to have a disability. What must follow is the teacher, who has far more power over the systems and culture within a classroom to then do the work of understanding difference and ableism and to help other students do the work of creating a classroom culture that is anti-WSCP.

This, then, is your first task. Before even getting your roster of students and a list of your students with learning disabilities, ask yourself, "How much do I understand about learning disability? What work have I done to decolonize my thinking around it? In what ways have I worked to create a classroom culture that highlights difference as an asset instead of a liability? What lessons, language, and work have I created to promote such a culture? Figure 2.4 lists ten more self-interrogating questions to help you get started. As you work through these questions, think about power in terms of race, appearance, sex, gender, ability, wealth, family, education, religion, language, job, mental health, body size, etc. You can think about your student population as a whole or narrow the scope to specific students.

FIGURE 2.4

Questions to Create an Inclusive Classroom

1. In what ways does my identity/experience align me with power/the system?
2. In what ways does my identity/experience misalign me with power/the system?
3. In what ways does my identity/experience differ from those I serve? How are their identities aligned/misaligned with the system/power?
4. How much education (formal or informal) have I had on critical pedagogy, political consciousness raising, liberation psychologies, ableism, disability history and disability studies, feminist studies, and other traditions/theories that critique the medical model of mental health/education? How can I continue my education in these areas?
5. In what ways do I see/observe/believe that systemic oppression interacts with education/mental health, and how do I tend to address this in my work/life?
6. In what ways do I practice humility when it comes to my work with differently abled kids? To what extent do I understand my authority as a teacher? In what ways do I see myself as the expert/norm?
7. In what ways do I perpetuate the system in place by aligning with it and its rights rather than the child's? (Try to come up with specific examples. Consider every time you ask a child to try to adhere to what the system considers acceptable/normal.)
8. In what ways do I act in solidarity and community with others around the issues that concern my students? (Try to think of specific acts–voting is not enough.)
9. In what ways do I actively resist the psychoeducational industrial complex? (Again, try to think of specific examples.)
10. What practical or political action have I taken to advocate/fight for the rights of my marginalized students? (This can include everything from speaking up for someone without a voice in a meeting to organizing campaigns.)

Sitting with questions like these is the first and most important step toward creating a horizontal classroom. Return to this list regularly—at the very least at the start and end of each term. When you feel ready, you can ask yourself what one thing you can do, either within or outside your classroom, to help shift your answer to one of these questions. This could be something as simple as reading a book or following a social media channel. Try to make this about actual shifts in your classroom. As you do this, also reflect on the process itself:

What examples did you think of?

What surprised you?

What angered you?

What embarrassed you?

What made you proud?

How did these feelings feel in your body?

How can these feelings relate to the way students feel/experience your classroom?

As you progress, try to move from one focus area a term to one a month. Doing this as part of a community of teachers can be even more powerful.

To study disability history is to trace the fault lines of power, where every aspect of WSCP converges to decide whose bodies count and whose minds matter. Ableism isn't just one "ism" among many. It's the foundation. When we study the history of how disability has been constructed, excluded, and resisted, we gain the tools we need to unlearn every system of oppression. In the roots of ableism, we find the roots of them all, and in its undoing, we find the possibility for truly liberatory education. This is why studying disability history is so important for every classroom teacher. So ask yourself, "What do I know of the history of disability and disability rights? What do I know about the ways in which able and neurotypical people have pushed against the basic rights of humans with disabilities? In what ways am I the recipient and ongoing agent of that history?" Figure 2.5 includes some additional questions to help you get started in learning about that history. These questions are drawn from numerous disability studies and disability justice scholarship, including works by Nielsen (2012), Heumann and Joiner (2020), Longmore (2003), Sins Invalid (2019), ADAPT (n.d.), Temple University Institute on Disabilities (n.d.), Baynton (2001), Mingus (n.d.), Disability Visibility Project (n.d.), Newnham and LeBrecht (2020), and ADA National Network (n.d.).

FIGURE 2.5

- What are the "ugly laws"? How do they continue to influence the ways in which we treat children with differences in neurotypical schools and classrooms?
- Who is Judy Heumann?
- Who is Ed Roberts? Why was polio as a disabling disease and not a congenital disability important? How does this relate to where we are today with COVID?
- What did disability rights advocates do after the Civil Rights Act passed without including people with disabilities?
- Where was Willowbrook (trigger warning if you decide to watch videos about this)? How does the legacy of institutionalization continue in schools today?
- Who is Brad Lomax? Why was MS as a disabling disease and not a congenital disability important here?
- What is the history of the 504 plan? How did it come to be? Why is it called that?
- In what ways did the civil rights movement and the disability rights movement intersect? Why is this intersection important?
- What is ADAPT, when did it come into existence, and what does it teach us about effective protest and resistance work?
- What is the Capitol Crawl Protest, when did it happen, and what does it teach us about effective protest and resistance work?
- What was *Olmstead v. L.C.*? Why is this case significant to schooling? How does it impact classrooms today?
- How did disability advocates and Senator Mitch McConnell clash in 2017? What does this teach us about our more current beliefs about disability? What does this teach us about the power of disability/

neurodivergence in defending the rights of able/neurotypical people and using disability to one's advantage?

- What does this history teach us about the concept of shame both as a tool for oppression and as a tool for emancipation?
- What ethical concerns are raised by all to track or list autistic individuals? What histories do these echo?
- How are terms like "data-driven," "personalized training," or "smart technology" being used in ways that subtly (or not so subtly) promote ableist standards?
- How does a technology like AI intersect with disability politics?

Remember, your goal is not to change the world. But your goal is to change *something*. Your true power lies in transforming the immediate—one moment, one decision, one choice at a time. Commit to one concrete thing per semester. Use the experiences that come up with your students to help you choose the most relevant action step. You are not here to conform to systems that were never built in love. You are here to disrupt, to unsettle, to question the very roots and foundations upon which everything is built. That is the work of teaching, and of learning. Speak these truths, and the answers to the questions you find. When you do, expect pushback. Don't let that throw you off. It's part of the process. It signals that you are changing the status quo. Revolution work is always slow and gritty. It is often lonely. It can take *years* before you feel any significant shifts. But every time you refuse to accept difference as deficit, you are part of a revolution against a system designed to erase, oppress, isolate, and diminish. Find ways to record your successes—maybe in a journal. Celebrate your small wins. When you are feeling demoralized, return to this to find the motivation to persevere. This is not extra work. It is the real work. And it begins wherever you are, with whoever is in front of you.

CHAPTER 3

CONNECTED EXPERIENCE

Olivia was referred to me just as she was making the transition from elementary to middle school. Her new public school, situated in a middle-class neighborhood in Los Angeles, had assured her parents that they would honor the 504 plan for her ADHD diagnosis that she had received two years prior. Olivia was a plucky, freckle-faced redhead with long, wild, tangled hair she could never manage to keep tamed. I remember the first time she sat her petite, round frame in front of me. Olivia had been using ADHD medication since her diagnosis but, as for many students, the medication was only slightly effective. Despite the side effects (mainly loss of appetite and some sleep issues), her parents felt the benefits to her ability to manage herself still made the medication worthwhile. What I noticed right away, and appreciated even though I knew she was struggling, was the stubborn spark in her eye that fortunately seemed unaffected by the medication. It matched perfectly with how unfazed she was by her backpack, filled with crumpled papers, random pens, and forgotten homework assignments.

I spent months working with her prescribing psychiatrist in hopes of trying alternatives. Olivia's mom, as well as her teachers, were concerned about how she was "managing herself"—like her backpack, her room was always a mess; she was being bullied at school about her hair and hygiene; and there were teachers reporting that Olivia never turned in work, even if she had actually finished it. It was unfortunate to hear her mom's report that her situation was an improvement over how she used to be.

What really struck me about Olivia's household, though, was that her room was not the only messy place in the house. ADHD ran in her family, her psychiatrist had told me, so Olivia was surrounded with chaos, with her mom regularly forgetting appointments, their house in a general state of disarray, and her parents struggling to support her while working full-time jobs that seemed to overwhelm them.

The only exception was Olivia's sister, Ava. Olivia was four years older than Ava, and the fact that her younger sister seemed to so easily navigate school and keep a clean room despite the chaos in their house was a point of shame for her. Every time I arrived at their house, I would watch as she ran past her sister's neatly organized room to her own and throw herself onto her spinning desk chair, which was eternally stuck, unable to spin due to the piles of clothes and bedding and old toys and garbage. "I don't know how she does it," she would sometimes say while holding her belly, as if just seeing Ava's uncluttered white desk and perfectly made bed caused her physical pain. "It's like she's the older sister or something," she would protest with a nervous laugh.

My attempts at helping Olivia clean her room would never last. There was never enough time, given the sheer amount of schoolwork and chaos in her room, and no matter what progress we made, the room would be a mess the following week. She had the same struggles organizing her backpack, her laptop, and her school agenda and calendar. While this is typical for kids with her profile, her struggles were exacerbated by the disorganization of her school. Every teacher seemed to be on a different platform and have their own system (Schoology®, Google Classroom, using an agenda, reading the whiteboard, etc.), and at every turn I was referred to the syllabus (which had no information on the ins and outs of navigating her classes). But I was regularly told "students have been taught how to navigate each course during class," which was of no help with a student like Olivia. Her teachers had no doubt repeatedly given her directions and reminders and she had repeatedly not listened or forgotten. Olivia and I would often have to spend the majority of our session time trying to figure out and find the work she needed to do. Turning her work in, of course, presented a whole other set of challenges.

Despite all this, Olivia was a conscientious student who really wanted to do well. She was an avid reader and loved and excelled in subjects like history, social studies, and English, though her grades didn't reflect her abilities. "I hate math," she had made clear to me from the very start though she was solid in her understanding of grade-level mathematical concepts. Outside of her executive functioning difficulties I could see no other learning-related issues, which made her C's, D's, and F's in the sixth grade especially unfortunate because she was clearly not able to demonstrate her abilities despite her 504 plan.

The one teacher Olivia had who was extremely organized and who had a very strict and regular curriculum and set of expectations was her English teacher. Following the district curriculum, this teacher had students work out of a specific workbook in which they were required to read passages, answer comprehension questions, and study vocabulary. The class routine was predictable. Each class, she assigned one passage that was due the next day and allowed to be corrected during class. Based on her 504 accommodations, this gave Olivia two extra days (based on the school scheduling system) to finish the five to six pages of questions and vocabulary words, a task so overwhelming and impossible for her that English class, and this particular assignment, had become the source of large-scale family breakdowns, screaming matches, and full-blown panic attacks.

Despite her two-day extra accommodation window, Olivia was forever playing catch-up in English, and her teacher refused to give her credit for work she tried to turn in more than one class session late. I originally thought the problem was Olivia's inability to plan and organize her time and stay on task until she finished the passages, but I came to realize the problem was more complex. Olivia wasn't able to ignore the hidden curriculum.

Like many other texts we still see in classrooms, the book Olivia studied from contained nonfiction passages that featured everything from history to astronomy. Olivia, I came to learn, would get stuck on the passages, especially the history ones.

"Why would the natives help people who have come over to take their land?" she would ask while reading a passage about Thanksgiving. "Why are they using the word *unpleasant* to describe what happened to Uncle Tom? Seems like that's a bit of an understatement," she would say while reading a passage about Harriet Beecher Stowe's pen being mightier than the sword. Excited to engage with her on these important questions, I would find myself responding to her critiques, encouraging her to ask more, even deeper questions. But soon I began to realize this was only hurting her grade more.

On one occasion, I remember Olivia dismissing the vocabulary review section of the worksheets and instead creating her own vocabulary map that changed the words used in the passage to words she felt fit better. The word *unpleasant*, for example, which she drew in a bubble with quotes, got connected to new bubbles that included words like *disgusting*, *unjust*, *inhumane*, *cruel*, *severe*, *savage*, and *tragic*, which, she declared, made a lot more sense when describing someone being beaten to death. She received a score of zero on this map, with her teacher writing "does not follow directions" in red marker above the page.

I had tried several times to email her teachers about the issues we were facing—I especially remember writing a strongly worded email to her English teacher after seeing the "does not follow directions" remark—but I never heard back. This is not atypical in public schools, where teachers can see up to 200 students a day and where students are expected to "self-advocate." Even parents' emails can go unanswered. But what was atypical (though some may disagree) was that the transition meeting with Olivia to middle school had not occurred by the time I met her in October of her seventh-grade year and, despite many attempts, we were not able to secure a meeting until after the New Year.

This not only meant that I never had a chance to introduce myself and Olivia to her teachers like I normally do in order to put her on their radar and further explain her needs; it also meant we lost a whole semester of schooling in which Olivia's teachers were not making any meaningful accommodations for her. For that entire semester, I essentially had to be her frontal lobes and help her turn in assignments, plan and organize projects, and study. What this soon translated to was me fighting Olivia and actually discouraging her from engaging with her work more deeply in order to just get it done and turned in. I will never forget the madness of trying to stop a curious, deeply critical student from thinking and engaging with her work in order to make sure she answered nonsense questions on time and in expected ways.

Olivia was one of the first students to ignite my own disillusionment with my job, though I have to admit she was not the last. I have regularly found myself pushing students to "get the work done" instead of wasting time thinking. The cognitive dissonance of participating in what Kliebard (1999) describes as the "school as a factory and the curriculum as a production process" in which students are "raw material" and the teacher "the overseer of the production process," making sure that the products are "constructed according to the specifications laid down and with a minimum of waste" (53) is something I had promised myself I would not normalize, but here I was, complicit in it.

EMPIRICISM

From our ontology, our epistemology grows. Epistemology, the study of knowledge, its sources, structures, and borders, looks at how knowledge gets created, justified, disseminated, and legitimized. Epistemologists are also concerned with how a person's knowledge of reality is essentially limited by the means and methods used to discern what is viewed as legitimate. Our ontology, what we believe about nature, gives rise to our epistemology, or how we believe we can come to understand nature and truth. In other words, what we believe to be true is shaped by how we believe truth is defined and proven—our way of being (ontology) shapes our way of knowing (epistemology). The epistemology of the West is empiricism. Empiricism is concerned primarily with observation, measurement, and ultimately, prediction. Western culture, which is shaped by WSCP ideology, prizes empiricism. Yet empiricism itself has a hidden curriculum: we all commonsensically assume it to be a requirement of truthfulness.

I teach a research methods course to graduate students studying to become psychologists and mental health professionals. Research methods is a standard course in most graduate programs in psychology and sometimes education. But we never ask, Whose methods? What type of research? It is assumed that the empirical research approach *is* research itself. In other words, empiricism, which is the epistemology of Western scientific thinking, is so all-encompassing that we assume it to be the only possible epistemology, or epistemology itself. But as I tell my graduate students, this is not the case. A science is a systematic way of knowing and interacting with the world. Science is not equivalent to empiricism. My students are often surprised to hear, for example, that there are such subjects as Indigenous science and Indigenous psychology and that these sciences are quite different from our own. Unlike empirical epistemologies that only consider that which can be observed and measured by human beings as knowledge, Indigenous epistemologies and therefore sciences take on ethical and moral dimensions (which cannot be measured empirically and are therefore excluded from empirical epistemology). They also begin from a place of seeing humans as part of an ecological system, and concepts like relationality and interconnection between sacred and secular are central to their sciences.

Another good way to think about epistemology is to think about language itself. Language shapes reality in the mind the same way that a positivist epistemology can shape what we consider scientific fact, or in the case of teachers, curriculum. As a bilingual person, I remember a discussion in our household as a child about the Persian (Farsi in the Iranian language) word *ta'rof*. I remember watching my mother struggle to explain the word to her American sisters-in-law, who were always shocked by why all their visiting Iranian family members were "so nice." Despite all her attempts, they couldn't really understand it. What's more, they kept offering a kind of pseudo-psychological critique, suggesting that being "too nice" is a sign of low self-esteem and that Iranians needed to stop doing this. I remember my mother mumbling in frustration after they left, something along the lines of "of course Americans with no culture can't understand this."

Ta'rof is not just a word in Farsi, it is a way of life. The word connotes elements of politeness, social hierarchy, and rules that are never stated but are so incredibly important to social interactions that I would argue they even rule the politics of a country like Iran. In other words, it is not a word, but in fact an epistemological formation that has evolved over time, perhaps in response to Iran's strategic and therefore dangerous geographic location in West Asia, carrying in it an entire way of thinking and being that is completely foreign to an individualist culture like America's. I understood my mother's statement that to not understand the concept is to lack culture and civilization entirely. And yet I could also understand how Americans viewed the idea as strange, which would sometimes lead to near fights in our family over who paid the bill at a restaurant or who walked through a door first.

But the word *ta'rof* and the epistemology it comes from—namely, one where the near destruction of the individual for the sake of the collective good and the willingness to suppress the ego self for the advancement of a loved one are considered highly valued traits—I think can help you better understand how vastly different social (and also educational) curriculums can evolve from different epistemological underpinnings.

To use Freire's term (2018), *naming the world* is directly linked to claiming it and to claiming those ways of viewing it that count as legitimate within the context of lived experiences. What better way to make an epistemology dominant than by literally removing the means by which one names the world, that is, their language? Given this, it should not surprise us to see the dark chapters in the history of American education (though of course not only the United States but all colonizing empires of the West) include the outlawing of Indigenous languages and cultures and the forced removal of Indigenous children from their families and cultures in order for them to be "educated" in "modern" schools by Western-thinking (superior) educators (Smith 1999).

In *Native Science: Natural Laws of Interdependence* (2000), the Tewa scholar Gregory Cajete emphasizes the differences between Western and Indigenous sciences. Instead of prioritizing objectivity, the lens of

Indigenous science is deeply relational and life sustaining, grounded in the interdependence, responsibility, and reciprocity with the natural world. Through the idea that we are participants in nature and therefore science, not just observers or manipulators, the hope of creating a more sustainable and meaningful world and future is embedded in the language and shapes what becomes its methodology. This is not to say that there is no observation or prediction in Indigenous sciences but that because the epistemology is not limited to those, a scientific system emerges that allows for the study of the interplay of nature with that which cannot be observed: the spiritual world. Feminist critiques of science like those of Haraway (1988) and Braidotti (2013) have long talked about the importance of "the politics of location" and "situated knowledge," arguing that the notion of "objectivity" often masks how dominant groups (meaning white, male, Western) have constructed knowledge that erases marginalized epistemologies. Thus, through Western approaches to schooling, even in the Islamic Republic of Iran, knowledge and epistemologies of subaltern populations have been systematically excluded and erased from the educational process and empirical science (Darder 2012).

Nowhere is this more relevant than in the classroom, where the battle over knowledge is played out by educators as they shape what counts as knowledge and where science is often treated as the ultimate authority without questioning how it excludes other ways of thinking and knowing, or epistemologies.

While we don't usually think of our curriculums as positivist or empirical, especially if we don't teach science, it is important to recognize that every curriculum in every classroom is shaped by the characteristics of positivism: linear, hierarchical, and therefore ableist. What's more, this is true all over the world. I spent the first five years of my schooling in Iran. But there, too, the curriculum and how it was delivered was based on Western epistemology and WSCP. Why? Because modern education itself is a tool of WSCP.

What this translates to in culture, including classroom culture, is a need for an outside measure to tell us we are good, we are smart, we are correct, we are of value, and ultimately that we deserve love. Therein lies the entire dynamic of traditional teacher-student and school-home relationships. Someone on the outside must validate our thinking. From that grows an entire system of "what is right," an ideal against which all is measured. Such thinking is what gives birth not just to white supremacy but also to the manifestations and ramifications of white supremacist thinking in educational settings—from race science, to phrenology, to IQ testing, to the theories and methods that form the basis of our modern education system and insist genetics, heredity, and inborn distinctions determine intelligence (Stephen Jay Gould beautifully unpacks this history in his 1981 *The Mismeasure of Man*). Teaching and schooling then become an effort to ever more perfectly observe and measure these distinctions. How many of us as educators mistrust our intuition and as a result teach our students to do the same? One could argue that the entire mechanism of Western schooling, steeped in empiricism, is training the body and the intuition to doubt itself and to instead learn to trust outside data and measures. The insistence to wait for data, for science, for outside information to validate or invalidate our intuition or instinctive impulse is the very basis of empiricism. This immediately places the mind both outside and above or over the heart and the body. Yang over yin. That is patriarchy, supremacy, and ultimately capitalism, which is an economic system based on hierarchical power.

No system has been used more globally to control knowledge than the Western education system. By presenting itself as the ultimate knowledge authority, built on specific ways of thinking shaped by dominant and exclusionary norms and values, science—and even pseudoscience—has systematically undermined other ways of knowing. This has helped shroud and eliminate conflicts that would have led to and catalyzed new knowledge paradigms and ways of understanding the world—paradigms that might challenge and question long accepted ideas and the power behind them. In other words, science is not actually taught as a field shaped by argumentation and counter-argumentation and evolving ideas, but as something neutral and objective, always hiding the moral, intellectual, and political struggles that have shaped it (Gouldner 1970). Students are therefore introduced to a scientific method that doesn't question its own goals, methods, or the assumptions it's built on (Dreeben 1968; Paraskeva 2011). In this way, science is no longer an ideology, but an objectively applied neutral force that ignores disagreements and is understood as the only path to progress all while limiting actual human capacity for knowledge building.

This is also directly in line with our mental health models, in which some measure outside ourselves (a psychologist or expert and/or a test or set of criteria) is employed to tell us if we are "sane," if we are "typical," if we are "normal," and again, if we are "worthy." Our power, our knowing, doesn't come from within, and our epistemology stems not from what the child shows or needs or knows but from the outside. We cannot depend on our intuition, on our inner knowing, or on our spiritual aspirations. Instead, we must lay ourselves bare on a surgical table and accept the value we are given after careful evaluation by some expert outside (note how this specifically impacts special education as a system).

Educational Hierarchies

My point here is not to say that science, or yang, is not of value. It obviously is. Rather the point is to show what happens when we create hierarchies where one oppresses or demonizes another or erases it all together, as empirical epistemology has. The term *epistemicide* (de Sousa Santos 2001, 2014) has been given to the genocide of all other epistemologies by empiricism such that today we no longer teach anything other than empirical science in schools the world over, rendering all epistemologies as subaltern, subordinate, and ultimately illegitimate. When we set up a worldview where empirical epistemology rules supreme, we become so out of balance that what results is a world where nature is burning, our mental health is declining, and the very future of life itself is at risk.

This is especially worrisome in fields like mental health and special education, where there is a push to bring together two systems of knowledge without allowing for engagement with the conflict that should and must arise from such a meeting. From an Indigenous perspective, for example, science is seen more as an abstract, symbolic, and metaphoric way of perceiving and understanding the world (Cajete 2000). This is in direct contradiction to the Western cultural perspective that views science as a rational way to solve problems. But these two approaches might share some complementary dimensions if they were allowed to exist side by side and engaged with horizontally. Cajete (1986) refers to "sacred twins in Native American mythology" and how they are by nature intimately interrelated. Dualities like light and dark, life and death, logic and intuition, are not opposites in conflict as they are in Western thinking. Instead, they are two parts of a whole, each deriving its meaning from the other.

Such a vision, however, is beyond our reach in the classroom, where the gap between research and practice persists because neuroscience aims to install the rational as supreme ruler within education. Cajete reminds us that, from an Indigenous perspective, science as a whole is based on *both* the intuitive and rational minds. This perspective moves more inclusively beyond the "boundaries of objective measurement" and honors the importance of "direct experience, interconnectedness, relationship, holism, quality, and value" (Cajete 2008, 491). These standards of Native American science are far more in line with the standards and values of an emancipatory education approach; and, more importantly, could work to transform the exclusions of Western science if it were to "allow for more holistic and integrated perception of itself to take hold and grow" (Cajete 2008, 496); and, as such, perhaps the bridge between neuroscience and education would no longer be a bridge too far (Bruer 1997).

Education theorist and critical educator Henry Giroux (1981) has noted that "American educational theory and research became firmly entrenched within an instrumentalist tradition that defined progress as technological growth and learning as the mastery of skills and the solving of practical problems" (5). In my experience, this is precisely the kind of educational theory that fields like special education wish to advance today. We are seeing more and more exact ways of measuring deficit in the child and the brain. I would say, for example, that over 80 percent of my clients now have a full neuropsychological evaluation to identify learning disabilities (at five to ten thousand dollars per evaluation) when such testing used to be reserved only for those with severe brain traumas and other medical issues. So we can see how this instrumentalist tradition is now even more engrained, not just in the new evaluative instruments made available by neuroscience and the *DSM*-5, but in the ways we are defining the very concept of learning, namely as the mastery of specific skills and the solving of practical problems as opposed to a "natural activity for all human beings [that is] lifelong and holistic" (Cajete 2008, 496).

While we think that all our advances in science and now neuroscience are somehow modernizing education, I would argue they are taking it backward. Herbert Spencer, who pioneered in the nineteenth century a functional curriculum design based on identifying and classifying human activities that became the predominant way of thinking within the US educational system, asked, "What knowledge is of most worth?" (Spencer 1860, 84). Neuroscience (as it manifests in special education today) still promotes his ideas about the goal of scientific knowledge and education as preparing individuals for "productive" roles in society. The Spencerian conception of a worthwhile curriculum has had major repercussions on the US curriculum for over a century (Paraskeva 2011), and special education today falls right in line with Spencer's (1860) vision:

> *Science. This is the verdict on all the counts. For direct self-preservation, or the maintenance of life and health, the all-important knowledge is—Science. For that indirect self-preservation which we call gaining a livelihood, the knowledge of greatest value is—Science. For the due discharge of parental functions, the proper guidance is to be found only in—Science. For that interpretation of national life, past and present, without which the citizen cannot rightly regulate his conduct, the indispensable key is—Science. Alike for the most perfect production and present enjoyment of art in all its forms, the needful preparation is still—Science, and for the purposes of discipline—intellectual, moral, religious, the most efficient study is, once more—Science. (84)*

This is still the push we see in education today. If science rules supreme, then our very methods of teaching and pedagogy must themselves be scientifically valid. Neuroscience then is not meant to learn along or with education; it is not even meant to simply impact it. There is, moreover, a quest to obliterate conflict between the two fields by assuming authorship and authority over education. We see today ways in which science is aiming to make its takeover of education even more complete.

This colonizing approach is found throughout the literature and language of education and especially special education. Science's imperialism was, ironically, born during the Enlightenment period and its modernity project and then facilitated by the Industrial Revolution (which transformed schools into assembly lines) as well as the philosophy of liberalism (with its focus on individualism), which determined Western scientific knowledge to be superior (Smith 1999). How, then, can modern neuroscience, which still has its roots in empirical epistemology, save education when nineteenth-century science set up the modern educational system specifically to discover, extract, appropriate, and distribute what it deems legitimate knowledge in an organized, excluding, and systematic way?

Here again is where teachers, in my opinion, need to push back, not at the notion of scientific evidence (like the science of reading for example), but at the notion of being ruled by empirical epistemology. If we aim to move forward in ways that actually tackle the problems faced by our educational system, we need to start by looking honestly at its history and how it has been shaped by colonialism, power, and control over knowledge. Instead of simply borrowing (or sometimes stealing—you be the judge in the Maslow example later) from Indigenous ways of knowing when it's useful, and then continuing to push dominant, colonial ideas, we need to recognize how the system has long worked to erase and replace other ways of thinking. As post-colonial theorist Edward Said (1978) argued—what we often call "neutral" is not neutral at all, but carries a hidden agenda and harkens *positional superiority*. What claims to be objective, reinforces the idea that Western ways of knowing are not just superior, but most damagingly, eventually, the only way, and that is part of the problem we must face and unlearn first as educators.

FAIR VERSUS EQUAL

When the meeting we had requested with Olivia's teachers finally did come, in mid-December, I felt desperate and angry. We had been given exactly twenty-five minutes for the meeting and only fifteen minutes before teachers had to return to class. After some administrative discussions, Olivia's teachers each shared their impressions. All of them had basically the same things to report: Olivia was bright and conscientious but disorganized. Some talked about her hyperfocus in certain classes, but she was often distracted, couldn't get her work in on time, in class or when assigned homework, and there seemed to be a general consensus that it was unfortunate that such a bright student couldn't get her act together and try to turn in work on time in order for her grades to reflect her abilities. This of course is the definition of a learning disability—a discrepancy between ability and performance—but since Olivia had no other learning disability, she did not qualify for an IEP and, as her English teacher again reminded, with a 504 plan she was only entitled to a couple of days for late work, extra time on tests, and preferential seating in class, all of which she was provided.

Before I had a chance to respond or share my impressions, the fifteen minutes were up and the teachers had to leave. This left me ten minutes, which meant I would not have the time to share anything meaningful, so I just went in for my ask: Could her teachers provide us with class lessons and materials in one compiled location so that I could have a way of knowing what is actually going on in class so we could cover the things she inadvertently missed during class time? And could she be allowed to upload or email work? Before the remaining staff had a chance to respond I rushed in with my final ask: Could we extend the deadline and just allow her to turn in work when it is done and still have it be graded without penalty so long as she got it in before the end of the term? If the purpose was to have her gain mastery and complete work, why not give her the actual time she needed? I tried as part of these quick asks to give an honest account of the frustration of the sheer amount of time we had to spend just figuring out where everything is and how things need to be done and turned in, and of work getting lost after being done, and of teachers refusing to accept late work and giving her zeros even when she did get work done and turned in.

With just four minutes remaining, I was told this was impossible. "Teachers simply don't have time to individualize like this for thirty students," the school vice principal proclaimed, though I wondered if all her teachers would have agreed had they still been in the meeting. "Learning executive functioning is a goal of middle school," she continued, "so Olivia will need to work on these skills. Also, under the 504 plan she already gets the max number of extension days, and we cannot legally change that." That's when her counselor chimed in, "Not to mention it would not be fair to other students." The vice principal nodded in agreement and added, "Since middle school is the time students are expected to learn these executive function skills, it would be an injustice to her to just bypass her. Best we teach her how to fish, don't you think?" she asked, proud of her analogy.

With less than a minute remaining I had no time to say that yes, I did agree that the middle school years are an important time to practice emerging executive functioning skills, except that wasn't happening. They didn't even have a comprehensive system for executive functioning among the teachers, and whatever time was being spent "explaining" the systems in the classroom, it clearly wasn't translating for Olivia. Instead, the meeting ended with the vice principal repeating that they were already giving her the maximum supports allowed under the law, that the "extra supports" I was asking for were not possible and, in her opinion, might actually be an impediment to getting Olivia ready for high school and beyond where she will have an even heavier executive function load. Olivia was in fact doing well enough, I was then told, and just "needed to focus" and "self-advocate and ask for help when she needed it."

I left the meeting feeling confused, defeated, full of shame—how I imagine Olivia usually felt at school—and convinced that I had to make sure Olivia never self-advocated and asked for help, like I had just done on her behalf, so that she was not met with the same responses.

Shortly after, the pandemic hit.

I was shocked, as I'm sure many others like me were also, to suddenly see the types of supports we as advocates had been asking for to no avail for years, decades even, suddenly become possible, as if overnight. Within a few weeks of the shutdowns, teachers were putting their lesson plans online in one location. Deadlines no longer mattered and students could turn in work when they could, with no penalty. Olivia didn't even have to log on to class and was allowed to do her work independently on her own time at her own pace if she wanted. If she did log on, she didn't have to bother with brushing her hair and tidying up her room, tasks that were difficult especially early in the mornings, as having the computer camera on was not required. If she missed something during class, she didn't need to worry. Teachers were uploading their notes and recording and posting lectures. It was as if the mass disabling of the pandemic had suddenly made everyone sympathetic to the trauma of navigating everyday life with ADHD. It was as if suddenly everyone had ADHD.

This has long been a core issue in disability rights. Fairness, in our ideology, is synonymous with sameness. When everyone suddenly needed these accommodations, there was no issue in allowing for them. But when only one person or a few people needed them, it was impossible.

When we shift from an individualistic to a collective ideology, we see that asking the entire class or school to provide an alternative for one can in turn help the entire collective down the line. When the pandemic hit, teachers were suddenly overwhelmed by how to move their curriculums online and teach virtually (my point here is not to diminish the heroic effort of teachers in doing this work but to encourage us to question why these shifts were made to seem impossible before). The truth is, the pandemic would have been easier on all teachers and students if we had learned the lessons differently abled kids had been offering for decades.

I remember thinking, "Who cares?" at Olivia's 504 meeting when I was told she did not qualify for the "accommodations" I was requesting. I didn't say it out loud, namely because these meetings are often so short that there is little time for questioning or advocacy. But when we choose justice over fairness the question really does become, "Who cares?" Who cares if she qualified? If it's something she needed that the school was capable of providing, why not do it? I know from many such meetings I have been to in my career that the response to "who cares?" is usually "Well, if we do it for one person, we have to do it for everyone," to which of course I would say great, let's do it for everyone. Many kids without any learning disabilities also benefit from the "accommodations" provided to some. This is of course at the heart of frameworks like Universal Design for Learning (CAST 2024) and the many other inclusion-based frameworks we have in education but can never truly put to work because the issue in education is less about what to do and more about why to do it. In fact, I would argue, we already know and have all the research on how to do things. The reason we don't is the why, and our why is colored by our ideology and our epistemology.

I've come to learn that sharing opinions like "who cares if she qualifies, let's just see what we can do to help" can earn you a reputation for being difficult or unreasonable among schools. But this is exactly what radical love looks like. Radical love does not begin by asking questions about fairness or even morality. It doesn't begin by asking questions about economics or budgets. Instead, it begins by asking questions about ethics. When we operate from a place of ethics, truth, and community, we tend to find a way, just as we all did when the pandemic hit. But when we disengage from the "why," we tend to get bogged down in boundaries around money and qualifications and diagnosis and expertise. Any caring, capable adult, which I know almost every teacher is, can figure out how to help a differently abled student. This is not to say that education or expertise in special education is not important. But just as our standards have turned to critical thinking and problem-solving as the markers of an educated mind, I would argue that any teacher is capable of researching and learning and experimenting and figuring out what their students need *if* they buy into the why. This "why" is determined by our ideology.

I hope you can see the connection to epistemology here. When our epistemology is rooted in empiricism, we are encouraged, in fact trained, to disconnect from the why. What results is a moving away from common sense. Common sense would dictate that as educators we would look to what our students need and try to provide it. Instead, we look to what the rules say about what our students are allowed and provide only that. This is the impact of Western positivist thinking and epistemology. When the trend began, for example, to push for STEM programs especially for girls and students of color, I remember thinking that only in a Western ideology would we push for teaching math and science in place of or at the expense of the humanities. The humanities teach us the "why" instead of just the "how" we learn in STEM. Is it any surprise that our epistemology, which should be concerned with the "why" of knowledge, simply disconnects from that and replaces it with the methodology alone?

FROM HIERARCHIES TO CONNECTION

What happens when we shift from practices that are rooted in hierarchy and measurement toward practices that are rooted in community and connection? I think the differences in Olivia's experience before and after the pandemic perfectly demonstrate this. After the changes that were put in place during the pandemic, Olivia's grades shot up within a few months. Her ADHD was not "cured." I still met with her regularly to help her. But the accommodations the school provided took away the biggest hurdles she had: managing time and space. Interestingly, these accommodations grew out of the connected experience and community the pandemic created by disabling all of us.

Herein lies one of the most important points about curriculum. A curriculum is not just content. To me, while the content of what we are teaching of course matters, the real difference is in the form and format of our teaching. The most antiracist, anti-ableist content, if taught using a "banking model" is still bad modeling. Rather, it is the flexibility and openness of both our curriculum and our pedagogy that matters most. A good question to ask ourselves as teachers is how we are delivering our curriculum. It may not seem so, but this is an incredibly political question and act. Education is itself a positivist enterprise, drowning under a crisis of curriculum and a call for reform that stems not from a lack of empirical evidence in the field, as we repeatedly hear today, but from the presence of the positivist tradition itself. In order for us to move toward a social justice paradigm, we need to understand that the ongoing, almost-epidemic call for reform in US education has far less to do with not having the ideal curriculum and much more to do with practices and curriculums that dehumanize students and teachers alike.

The ask for Olivia to have her assignments along with directions listed and for her to be allowed to work at her own pace, without deadlines and penalties, may not seem like a big deal, but to me the issue gets at the very heart of social justice. It has been argued that the struggle for social justice is a struggle to achieve cognitive justice (de Sousa Santos 2007) and to democratize knowledge (Paraskeva 2011). In the same way that people with physical disabilities have had to fight for access to things like voting rights despite the disabilities that keep them from appearing in person to vote, so too does the student with a learning disability that prevents them from planning and organizing and meeting deadlines deserve equal access to the grading structures that then give them access to other rights and privileges. This is not to say that we do not work on executive functioning skills or that we have no other ways to check in to ensure a student is keeping up with class requirements, but to impose our concepts of time on a brain that processes time completely differently is ableist and socially unjust.

In Olivia's case, it took a kind of revolution, a mass connecting event (the pandemic) to bring about the changes she needed. When the pandemic happened, the way curriculum was delivered changed at the roots because for a moment in time, our epistemology was able to shift at the roots, from empiricism to connection.

To further help unpack the differences between an epistemology rooted in empiricism versus connection, I often draw the attention of my graduate students to Abraham Maslow. Maslow's hierarchy is one of the most well-known and widely used frameworks in psychology. But when I tell my students that Maslow's hierarchy was actually "inspired" by Blackfoot teachings and that this framework reflects an example of epistemicide (Blackstock 2014; Huitt 2007; Ravilochan 2021), they are often surprised.

The triangle, or pyramid, we all know so well with physical needs at the bottom and self-actualization at the top is actually the reverse of the Blackfoot's perspective (Ravilochan 2021). In the First Nations framework, self-actualization is at the bottom, as anything to do with "self" is considered a lesser level of consciousness. Above that is community actualization, and at the very top is what is translated as cultural perpetuity. I can only imagine poor Maslow, steeped deeply in positivist epistemology, trying to make heads or tails of a framework with multiple dimensions of reality and infinite time, which was part of the First Nations perspective. Instead, I can see him, after just a few short weeks of living with the Blackfoot Nation, desperately trying to categorize things in a linear hierarchical framework that is based solely on individual needs and rights and limited to one lifetime. Also of note is that Maslow went to live with the Blackfoot tribe because he wanted to test his theory that social hierarchies are maintained through the dominance of some over others. He was shocked instead to find high levels of cooperation and minimal inequality and high levels of life satisfaction and self-esteem among all the tribe members, thus proving his theory wrong. He was also shocked that "success" was measured by the tribe and prestige given not to those who had the most but to who had the least, because they had chosen to give away the most. Similarly, he was surprised to find that they did not view "self-actualization" as something we strive toward, but rather as innate to everyone at birth. In other words, everyone is trusted to be the best version of themselves already; this is not something they have to learn about or work to achieve, as in his appropriation of the framework. Things like basic physical needs, safety, and conditions for the expression of purpose were also all seen as a community responsibility, not something any individual had to secure for themselves. In the First Nations perspective, the aim is multigenerational Community Actualization and Cultural Perpetuity, never on an individual level. Human needs, they understood, are not hierarchical nor independent. They are interdependent and holistic (Anderson and Blue 2016; Blackstock 2011; Taylor 2019; Rathunde 2011).

Maslow never published what his research actually showed and what he really learned about human development and life satisfaction from the Blackfoot tribe, perhaps partially because of the risk of dismissal due to racism. My own view, however, on why Maslow not only did not report his findings but rather went a step further to essentially steal and then shift the First Nations framework into an individualistic one is epistemology. Is Maslow's hierarchy a framework for human development, or is it a white man's reflection of human development steeped in his own inability to escape Western thinking?

What we consider knowledge, which is based on Western scientific research, is primarily based on research that is more than 70 percent sampled from American undergraduate students and centers Western thinking as cognition itself (Watters 2013; Henrich 2020). As the cultural anthropologist and researcher Joseph Henrich and his colleagues have argued, American college students are the WEIRD-est people in the world (Westernized, Educated, Industrialized, Rich, Democratic), making them an invalid sample for scientific research that we then generalize to all of humanity. I encourage every educator to read into this fascinating body of literature. (Nisbett's work on the differences between Western and Asian cognition and the role of geography in these differences is also eye opening.) It shows not just the shortcomings and lack of validity in Western epistemologies but also that scientists are not immune to interpreting the world based on their own lens and seeing it as a reflection of their own thinking. Empiricism, for all its insistence on observation and measurement and neutrality, is no more immune to culture and ideology than any other epistemology (it may interest you to know that Henrich and his colleagues received huge backlash from the scientific community when their research first suggested that the WEIRD issue brings all empirical research under question). This is how our epistemologies shape our world view. They give rise to our scientific questions, theories, and research and ultimately how we construct knowledge and understand the world.

I don't say all this to create a hierarchy and put empirical epistemology at the bottom. Empiricism with its limited, linear thinking has given us much in the way of progress. However, because of that same limited, linear thinking it has failed to comprehend and account for the ramifications of much of that progress. The point then is not to make any one epistemology bad or dangerous but to emphasize the importance of allowing multiple ways of thinking and seeing the world to coexist, all with their own inherent value and place in the larger mosaic of our asymptotic relationship with knowledge and knowing. The point is to acknowledge that students who need accommodations (more time, written instructions, lecture notes, etc.) are as equally entitled to a classroom that allows them to learn as are students whose brains work within the traditional confines of schools.

Rhizomic Curriculum

I came across the term *rhizomic* in my first neuroscience class at the University of Pittsburgh. Our professor, a famous neuroscientist but not so great teacher, would regularly talk about the "rhizomic nature" of neuronal connections. I never looked up the term—there was no time to learn even the actual neuroscience terms in the class—and I never came across it again until reading a book for my doctoral thesis on curriculum. This time I did look up the word and its history, but it was not until watching a zombie show years later where people were being killed by a rhizomic system of fungi that I visually understood the term (it is only now that I'm realizing the similarities between fungal rhizomes and neurons in the brain!—see Figures 3.1A and B). Let me explain it here to help distinguish it from the idea of a linear and hierarchical curriculum, which is the curriculum of most schools in our neurotypical culture and the type of curriculum I hope we can move toward in the rhizomic thinking of neurodivergence.

FIGURE 3.1A

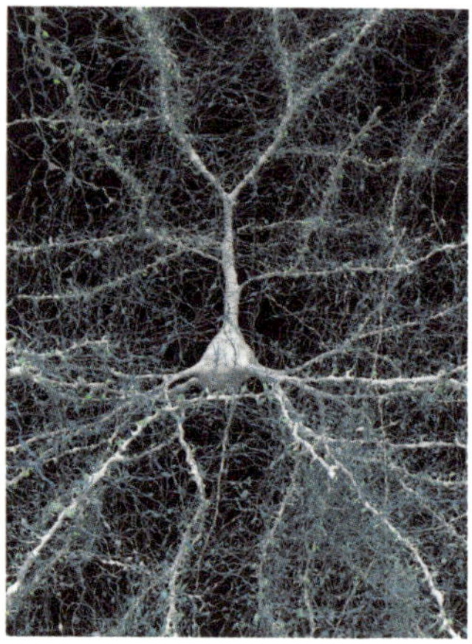

FIGURE 3.1B

The notion of the rhizome in terms that can apply to curriculum and learning and knowledge construction was first introduced by the French philosophers Gilles Deleuze and Felix Guattari in their text *A Thousand Plateaus* (1987), in which they make a distinction between what they call a *rhizome* and what they call *arborescence*. They say that a rhizome structure is like a root system that does not follow any set plan; it is spontaneous and chaotic. It pursues its own routes based on what it's interested in doing. It is a system that fundamentally opposes any kind of traceability. This is in opposition to what they call an arborescent structure, which does not embrace multiplicity and difference and possibility but instead has settled upon itself and just exists as itself. An example of this is a tree, a solid standing structure that does not move. While in a rhizomatic system there might be moments when there is the right concentration of water and energy, in response to which the rhizome will form into a bulb and become something like a potato, such a structure is ever moving, ever changing, ever growing in response to environment. They make this distinction to say that as human beings we are in fact much closer to rhizomes than to trees. Deleuze and Guattari specifically used this to oppose Freudian psychoanalysis, which they claim essentialized humans to an arborescent structure (where everything is just about parents and psyche), but it is not hard to see that this is true in all Western scientific thought and knowledge. Western scientific thinking has reduced us, all life, to the idea of a tree—without chaos, without mess, without the constant sense of unknowing.

The most fundamental way in which this impacts teaching and curriculum is in the way science, despite all the new rhetoric about neuroplasticity and growth mindset, has reduced, equated, and mistaken the brain for the mind. In this thinking, all human consciousness is seated in the brain, an organ that can be observed and measured. Consciousness, which cannot be measured, is then denied as existing separate from the brain. If you have ever wondered why all diagnoses in the *DSM*-5 are based on observable behavior instead of the inner experience of the "patient," this is why. If you have ever wondered why we still cling to the "chemical imbalance" model of mental health, despite robust scientific evidence showing that low serotonin is not the root cause of depression, this is why (Moncrieff et al. 2022; Kirsch et al. 2008). Our epistemological mistake, our conversion of rhizomic beings into arborescent ones, has made it so we are missing a whole and very important part of the picture altogether. This other part, this energy, soul, spirit, chi, mind, whatever you want to call it must be deleted because it cannot be observed or measured. When we begin with equating the mind and the brain (as Descartes did), we end with a system that aims to medicate children into conformity because of a "chemical imbalance" and force them into ableist conformities of trees when they are in fact neurodivergent rhizomes. While we'll unpack how our epistemologies create invalid tools and methodologies for diagnosis and treatment like the *DSM*-5 or our teaching curriculums, it is important to see that the epistemological shifts we must make can actually begin with changes to our curriculums and the ways we run them.

In Olivia's example, I view the question of "why" as one that arises from honoring the human and allowing a rhizomic curriculum to emerge as a result. When Olivia would come up to something in her reading that made her mind go in a different direction, in a rhizomic curriculum she would have the opportunity to do so. I would not have to keep returning her to a linear curriculum in hopes that she would get points and get better grades. Instead, there is enough creative space for the connections in her mind to occur as they want to. A rhizomic curriculum would be one that welcomes her critical thinking and all the tangents it needs in order to evolve. This is how we allow the minds of expert scientists and artists to work. In fact, to be a scientist or an artist is to push against the boundaries of linear thinking and allow the mind to follow and reflect the rhizomic nature of nature's ever-expanding curriculum. But we do not do this in school even though we claim we want to raise future scientists and artists. Why? In my opinion, this is because of Western empirical epistemology and the limitations it places on human thinking.

CONNECTED EXPERIENCE

In *Ideology, Culture, and the Process of Schooling*, Henry Giroux (1981) claims that "the task of radical educational theory is to identify and move beyond those classroom structures which maintain an oppressive hidden curriculum" (82). The radical core of any pedagogy, Giroux argues, "will be found not in its insistence on a doctrinal truth as much as in its ability to provide the theoretical and structural conditions necessary to help students search for and act upon the truth" (86). How do we, as individual teachers but also as school communities, push back and resist these hidden curriculums?

If the first step toward social justice education is to cultivate the capacity to be critical (Freire 2018), the second step, after taking a decolonizing lens to our own experiences, positionality, and beliefs (our ontology), is to begin to audit our epistemology, our curriculums, and our classroom structures.

For a rhizomic curriculum to take hold, it must be based on a centerless, periphery-less position (Paraskeva 2011; Deleuze and Guattari 1987; Eco 1984). To do this, as educators we have to commit to fight for a decolonizing praxis in which we push toward "instability, not stability" (O'Brien and Penna 1999, 106) and embrace the conditions of the messy, non-Western scientific world of education.

Again, to me, curriculum comes down to two things: content and form. This means we need to see if the diversity of the students we have is reflected in both the content and the form of the curriculum. This requires some level of understanding of our students, their histories, their differences, their needs, their interests, and their limitations. But generally, we can take any curriculum, whatever standards it needs to meet, whatever subject it teaches, and examine it along lines of form and content. The aim is for our curriculums to be both

1. representative/relevant in content, and
2. flexible (rhizomic) in form.

This examination will happen at different levels for different teachers. If, for example, you have never considered issues of content and form, the changes you make might be simpler to start. You may want to begin with small questions like the following:

> If mastery is the goal, why would it be unfair for my students to turn in their work when they are ready?
>
> What is the value of strict deadlines? How do these deadlines impact the experiences of my students?
>
> What are my values? Is it more important for this student to learn how to meet deadlines right now, or is it more important for them to be able to relax into the work, to grow with it, without the anxiety of looming deadlines?
>
> Is it impossible for this student to keep to deadlines because of their disability?

You can ask similar questions about all elements of your curriculum. For example, if you assign a specific format for students to construct their assignment, is it more important for them to follow that format or to demonstrate their comprehension and mastery of the content? For teachers who have already done considerable work around creating more flexible systems for students, the question might be how a curriculum can be shifted to make it more rhizomic. How can there be opportunities for students to make the curriculum their own?

The same is true for content. What are ways students can access the curriculum in ways that reflect them? This can be as simple as providing a book list that reflects your students' diverse identities and allowing them to choose, or it can be more advanced, like allowing them to create their own curriculum, with benchmarks and research that they deem valuable and important to them.

This is the step that most classroom teachers have immense expertise in. The point is to ask ourselves how our curriculum design will change if we center difference in it. This means that we ourselves have to first let go of the idea of a curriculum that is concrete and arborescent and instead allow it to be less known, more fluid, and more changeable throughout the semester. Such an approach is directly in line with all the proven theories about learning. It tends to be the approach we have when students are slightly younger and we are more willing to accept a play-centered approach for their learning. But this approach does not change from a developmental perspective as kids get older. Humans learn best through free play and self-directed experience at every age. To what extent does your classroom and curriculum create a container for this? To what extent does it stifle it?

It is important for me to note, as an educational therapist, that sometimes the answer to the question of what is more important actually *are* the deadlines and executive functioning skills. Sometimes what students need is more rigid structure. Olivia, for example, desperately needed the pressure of the classroom deadlines to be lifted, but she still benefited from ongoing weekly accountability sessions that helped her continue to make progress. With this approach she was not regularly penalized (and also not completely stressed out) for missing deadlines despite the two-day extension her 504 accommodations allowed (which was never enough), and she was able to finish all her work weeks in advance of the end of the semester.

I think one of the greatest teachings of kids with ADHD/AuDHD* is the different ways we can process and experience time. Our view of time in the education system is still very linear and Newtonian. Of course, modern physics has upended all that. What I often find difficult to process, like many of the students I talk to, is the discrepancy between what is being taught and how, such that we may even be teaching students quantum physics, all the while expecting them to operate under the laws of a completely outdated universe. But we don't need to have a quantum understanding of time to create meaningful structures for our students. We need only to watch them, or ourselves, in good faith. Every one of us carries all the wisdom of the universe.

*AuDHD is a term used to describe individuals who have both autism spectrum disorder (ASD) and attention-deficit/hyperactivity disorder (ADHD).

CHAPTER 4

CONTEXTUALIZED DIAGNOSIS

Imani was referred to me at the start of her eighth-grade year, shortly after completing a full neuropsychological evaluation. Her mother told me this testing had been "suggested" (but really required) by her private school in the Pacific Palisades, which she attended on scholarship and where teachers had become increasingly concerned with Imani's inability to keep up with her schoolwork. The results of her evaluation indicated a range of processing issues as well as a diagnosis of a language-based disorder and ADHD. The report also noted that as a Black girl in a primarily white school, Imani might face some "cultural tensions." Outside of some developmental and basic family history, that was the extent to which her history and her positionality were addressed. The remainder of the report presented scores on the testing, academic issues since first grade, a classroom observation, and a discussion of the diagnosis, along with recommendations that included educational therapy. The report also emphasized that, while an eager and conscientious student, Imani may not be a good fit for the school's rigorous curriculum and that school placement should continue to be a topic of discussion. I could not agree more. Not because I agree with the idea that a school should be able to tell a child "they don't fit"—isn't it after all the job of a school to reach out to and provide services to every member of its community?—but because I knew that this school, like many other "progressive" private schools on the west side of Los Angeles, promoted itself as inclusive and diverse (Imani's picture was featured on the cover of their main promotional flyer!), but actually followed a very traditional model and curriculum without any real knowledge of learning differences.

What really stood out to me about Imani's report were the accounts from her teachers indicating that Imani was usually asleep during class. This information was used to help support her ADHD diagnosis with an inattentive subtype—a diagnosis I didn't necessarily disagree with based on my own impressions of her. With every student, however, I do my own intake before reading their report. Imani was tall for her age. Her frame was so thin I had wondered if her medication might also be impacting her appetite. But there was no report of that. When I met her at her house for the intake, she was alone. I was struck by how shy and soft-spoken she was as she showed me around her home. Along with her mom, she lived in a two-bedroom condo in a luxury building near the water. But what I also learned that day was that Imani's older sister and her one-year-old son also lived with them.

Although like many other students I had worked with at that school and across Los Angeles, Imani lived in a wealthy neighborhood on the west side of the city, I remember walking into her unit and being surprised by how small it was. Compared to the extravagant lobby, and in comparison to the homes I was often in, it was an unusually small apartment. Little was revealed in the report about the family's finances. I knew her mother worked and that her father, though not in the picture, helped a bit with her school tuition. Imani stood taller than me, her dark brown eyes wide and unsure. She was quietly striking, the kind of beautiful that didn't yet know itself. But in that building, she looked just as uncomfortable as she had on the cover of the school magazine. And just like on the cover, she looked sad.

Other than size, I was also struck by how clean the apartment was. My experience visiting the homes of students with ADHD (which tends to run in families) had prepared me for chaotic and busy homes with little in the way of organization or systems in place. But Imani's apartment was squeaky clean, uncluttered, and meticulously organized. Even the small room she shared with her sister, which included a crib and three other large pieces of baby furniture in addition to a double bed, was perfectly neat. There was no desk, no bookcase, no evidence that a school-aged child lived in that room, or anywhere in the apartment. But nothing was out of place.

Unlike many kids with ADHD, who can feel overwhelmed with the intrusion of someone into their space, Imani was calm and polite as she showed me around. She even asked me if I would like a glass of water as we took off our shoes before entering the house. Her posture stiffened and she shifted her weight from one foot to the other, visibly uncomfortable, when I asked if I could see her workspace. She seemed embarrassed by the baby furniture and kept telling me her sister was only with them temporarily. Seeing her discomfort as she struggled to create a space at the kitchen counter for us to work, I suggested we go downstairs to the business center I had seen in the lobby—a good idea, she said, that had never occurred to her. When I expressed my surprise at how neat her room was, Imani's shoulders fell. "You should have seen it before," she said, looking down. "It's so hard to keep it clean now, but I try. My mom helps me too, but it's hard. That baby is so messy." When we finally settled in at the conference table in the business center downstairs, I asked Imani if she could utilize this space for her homework. She said she couldn't because often when her sister was home she needed help with the baby and Imani needed to be there. She also said she didn't know where their key to the conference room was (I had had to ask the doorman to let us in as a favor that day) and that she didn't want to bother her mom about it. And, she added after I offered to talk to her mom about the key, some of her friends lived in the same building and she wouldn't want them to see her working there and asking questions. Still, she agreed that while you could hear the noise from the lobby in the business center, the large clear table and the spacious room felt inviting. "Maybe I'll try to work here," she finally said, "we'll see."

I had no issues getting a meeting at Imani's school. In fact, the school staff were very eager to meet about her. They prided themselves on having structures in place that allowed everyone to come together for their SCSs, or student-centered success meetings, as they called them. Within a week of my request, I attended a meeting that included eleven people in total—all her teachers, the school counselor, the learning specialist, the dean of student affairs, and the principal, as well as me and Imani's mother. I was shocked. Imani, ironically, was missing from the "student-centered success meeting." I was assured that this was only because they wanted to discuss things with me first and that the learning specialist and counselor would relay everything to her later and be sure to answer any questions she had.

Race was the first thing I noticed when I got to the school—aside from the science teacher and the principal, the entire school staff was white. I knew from reading their profiles that both the Black science teacher and principal were alumni of the school, which I found interesting. And then there was me and Imani's mother. Each teacher took their time talking about what a wonderful person Imani was: polite, thoughtful, kind . . . but tired. They all seemed well versed in describing ADHD symptomatology and very understanding of the needs of "differently abled" children.

"Children with ADHD are more likely to have sleep disorders," Imani's evaluator had written in the report, "and the severity of their sleep problems correlates with their ADHD symptom score." Imani did in fact have ADHD. Her processing and language delays (though not significant enough to qualify her for a second diagnosis) also posed challenges for her. But the real reason she couldn't keep her eyes open in class was far simpler. She wasn't getting enough sleep. Any teacher would wonder if a student who is tired in class might be sleep deprived. But because Imani had a diagnosis, the simpler explanation was ignored.

As I reviewed her scores, I found myself thinking of the concept of WEIRD (Henrich et al. 2010; Henrich 2020; Watters 2010, 2013) and how assumptions tied to able-bodiedness and neurotypicality shape the standards by which assessments are normed. Generalizing data from a WEIRD population to the whole of humanity is like studying penguins to generalize about birds, I had read. What does it mean when we study typical learners and generalize to all learners?

In my research methods class, I have students watch a TED Talk called "Different Ways of Knowing" (Tammet 2011). In it, Daniel Tammet, a savant who is autistic, describes how his linguistic, numerical, and visual synesthesia impacts the way he sees numbers in his mind, which is different from most of us. I then invite my students to discuss the ramifications of our academic (and social) classroom norms being set by neurotypical people who not only see numbers the same way but assume everyone sees them the same way. I then ask them to think about other differences we might have in a classroom. And then, circling back to our discussion of WEIRD populations, we talk about missing entire ways of knowing, thinking, and understanding. The narrow lens we take to the human experience, all the while claiming to have the only legitimate lens, doesn't just erase entire ways of knowing and thinking, but the actual experience of every unique human being who comes to us in search of healing and guidance. Narrow epistemologies lead to narrow methodologies, and I think about this every time I read a neuropsychological evaluation report.

DEDUCTIVE METHODOLOGIES

As Stephen Jay Gould beautifully traces in his 1981 book, our current systems of testing, which include diagnosis in special education, emerged as the methodology of empiricism. It is to be expected that an empirical epistemology that focuses on observation yields a categorization and diagnostic methodology aimed at diagnosis using deductive reasoning to draw conclusions about behavior. In many ways, the *DSM*-5 is the core of our methodology in both psychology and education, as it not only labels and classifies all mental states, but also and more importantly presents a rubric for diagnosis. Practically every diagnostic criterion reads as the observations of an external observer and not the self-reporting of a "patient" about their inner state. Interestingly, self-report is considered the least reliable data in psychology even though no one is experiencing the inner state but the self. Yet, as developmental psychologist Urie Bronfenbrenner notes, the criteria used to assess students are derived from generalizations deducted from the strange behavior of children in strange situations with strange adults (Bronfenbrenner 1979). Students are rarely assessed in their natural environment; instead, a specialist whom they've often never met before observes them in an environment that is sometimes even artificially constructed to "standardize" the assessment. Most teachers or psychologists would comfortably admit that our behaviors are often responses to our environment and cannot on their own be a description of our inner experiences and feelings.

Herein lies the shaky and fundamentally invalid ground on which mental and psychological science and diagnosis lie: We talk about diagnosis as if the observable behaviors represent some inherent inner identity of the person when all they signify are their behavioral reactions and responses as mediated by their inner mental state, of which we have zero understanding because it cannot be observed by an outside observer. And while it may seem that we in education are somewhat safe from this lack of validity since the special education criteria do not use the *DSM*-5 in the school system but rather the Individuals with Disabilities Act (IDEA) law, the fact is, IDEA is also a diagnostic methodology based on exactly the same observational principles as the *DSM*-5. This also impacts our methodology in education in general, where testing, be it standardized or any other kind, is used to determine what a student knows in their head. The problem is, test-taking itself is a limited methodology that often leaves teachers unable to truly gauge what a student knows. I cannot count the number of times I have had students, Imani included, not be able to demonstrate their knowledge due to test anxiety, language confusion, and a whole host of other reasons, making test results an invalid representation of student understanding. And this isn't limited to tests. In 2022, in response to the proliferation of AI in educational settings through tools like ChatGPT, many critics, like Stephen Marche lamented the consequences of the proliferation of AI. In his article, "The College Essay Is Dead," Marche helped catalyze the critique of AI by arguing that the ability to write an essay is the quintessential test of an educated mind (Marche 2022). Never mind that this kind of linear, five-paragraph essay is extremely disabling for kids with executive function disorders like ADHD who may otherwise be extremely intelligent, or that "worship of the written word" is actually a tenet of white supremacy (Okun n.d.). My point here is not to degrade the importance of being able to write. I am a writer myself. But I also know from years of work with kids with disabilities that how I can think and deduct in linear sentences in my mind in order to get my thoughts across is not how others think, and what comes naturally to me and can therefore be shaped in our current schooling models is not generalizable to everyone. Our methodologies in schooling are, by empiricism's own standards of validity, invalid. So what do we do?

Once again, we can rely on Indigenous sciences to guide us away from the corners into which we seem to push ourselves with our limited lens. Instead of valuing abstract knowledge derived from experiments and controlled variables, Indigenous sciences acknowledge that knowledge is derived through direct interaction with the natural world and that research encompasses all processes of perceiving, thinking, acting, and coming to know that evolve through human experience. Human beings, students included, are part of a system, a history, and an ongoing process. In this way, every student, every diagnosis, becomes an opportunity for critiquing the medical model that shapes not only our special education system, but education in general. This is also why I believe that children with disabilities in our school system hold the key to the undoing, and therefore the healing, of our schools. In fact, I would argue that if you pulled at the thread of any and every issue in your school system, you would arrive at the issue of ableism and the question of how we see and treat difference as the central issue to address. This is why I strongly believe that if we listened to the needs and asks of students with differences, we could build systems and schools that work better for everyone.

With regard to methodology, we need to question the most holy concept in Western medicine and mental health: that of diagnosis and disease. We need to question why inclusionary pedagogical practices for diverse learners continue to be lacking from the point of view of misdiagnosis and incomplete diagnosis. We need to take the opportunity to use a student's diagnosis to ask larger questions about the merits of making education more "scientific," the value of the ever-evolving tools of measurement now coming in from neuroscience into education, and whether the problem is not that our tools are not exact enough, but rather that we cannot measure teaching or learning using such tools at all. In this way, the diagnosis sees the student as part of a system, a history, and an ongoing process.

CONTEXTUALIZED DIAGNOSIS

In most school meetings, I find myself making a case for the child's diagnosis, trying to help the school understand that the behaviors they are observing (failing, not doing homework, spacing out, apathy, outbursts, etc.) are due to the child's diagnosis and are "normal" behaviors given the student's learning profile. At Imani's school, however, things were different. All her teachers had received professional development from the learning specialist at the school and accepted Imani's diagnosis of ADHD. They assured me and Imani's mother that they were here to support Imani any way they could. It was important to them that she did not equate her worth with her academic achievement. Based on her teachers' reports, she was regularly groggy and tired during classes, sometimes even taking naps, but "we understand that is a symptom of her inattentive ADHD," the learning specialist assured us. "Don't worry, the teachers know not to penalize her for that."

My intuition, like that of Imani's mother's, was that in *this* case, her ADHD was being used as a scapegoat by her school. Imani's mother had expressed to me before the meeting that the school did not require enough accountability from Imani. She wished Imani faced more consequences. "Well, I sometimes tell her she needs to sit up," objected Cherylynn, Imani's science teacher, in a low, hesitant whisper.

When Imani's mom had to leave the room to take a call during the meeting, I took the opportunity to ask the group, "Do you think the tiredness might be due to her nephew and room situation?" They had no idea what I was talking about. I explained that Imani was not getting enough sleep because she shares her room with her young nephew. "There was nothing noted in the report about sharing a room or living with family!" the learning specialist exclaimed.

Imani's case is a perfect example of why it's so important to know the student independent of their diagnosis. Even at a school that seemed to have all the language and even the structures for centering students, it seemed that the story of the diagnosis trumped the student's own story. Diagnoses, especially ones like ADHD, can have very similar symptomatology to many other things, and sometimes to issues that are not diagnostic at all.

None of this is to say that diagnosis is not important. I have seen confused teachers, therapists, and parents working to remediate the wrong issue in children countless times. Diagnosis is a necessary part of the process, first because for better or worse it is what allows the child to get the services they need and deserve. Second, it is always easier to look toward something when you have a map and an idea of what you are looking for. So, diagnosis is important. It's just not doctrine. It must be understood within the complex history and context that it comes in.

Disability as a Social Construct

Many students come to the school environment with a diagnosis (please keep in mind that you may have *many* who don't but still need support). It is imperative that we understand these diagnoses beyond the basic "accommodations" that we feel obligated to know and even beyond the descriptions and definitions given by the *DSM*-5 and IDEA. We need to remember that all these diagnoses are based on standards of "normal" that are culturally and socially constructed.

Unlike a medical condition such as hypertension, for example, where you can point to a measure and show it is the same across all cultures, many mental health and disability diagnoses are a grouping of observed behaviors that *we* named. It's true that we can point to research that shows they exist in all cultures, but that is still based on us applying our thinking and metrics and language to a different culture. In fact, these diagnoses change even within our own culture. A clear example of this is homosexuality. Regardless of what your beliefs are, the fact is that homosexuality used to be considered a mental health disorder in the *DSM* and no longer is. This change was not due to any changes in "symptoms" but rather a social decision about whether homosexuality is a disease or not. This was not a change that occurred as a result of more scientific understanding. Our understanding of what cholesterol levels in our bodies mean might change, but that is not the same as a diagnosis being based on social norms, norms that are in fact set by WSCP.

Critical educators have long pushed back against our current medical models of special education being too entrenched in empirical and medical assumptions (Connor et al. 2008; Dudley-Marling and Burns 2014; Smith et al. 2009). Our current models, with medical and psychometric testing at the heart, see the disability as a deficit within the child (Connor et al. 2008) and constantly attempt to refine diagnostic and therapeutic interventions in hopes of remediating or curing children from their ailment (Skrtic 1991; Smith et al. 2009). The heavy reliance on testing and diagnosis of children has been less about understanding the child and more about appropriately placing them at best with the intention of predicting, diagnosing, controlling, and fixing students and at worst marginalizing and segregating them when they are not able to fit in the dominant system of education (Slee 1998). It was this criticism, along with new research findings, that showed not only overrepresentation but also misrepresentation of students of color and English language learners in special education (Artiles et al. 2002; Artiles and Trent 1994; Connor et al. 2008; Skrtic 1991) that prompted the shifts in the field toward mainstreaming and inclusion (Osgood 2005). However, these shifts have not resulted in much meaningful change in terms of the traditional model. Many critics continue to insist that the current system must be reexamined in the context of larger cultural and political processes and power differentials (Brantlinger 2006). Arguing that schools often represent a culture of power, critical educators have pointed out that special education's "scientific" and hierarchical practices replicate not just larger societal injustices but actually promote neurodeterminism and ableism (Connor et al. 2008).

But people have long resisted these practices. Disability studies, for example, were established and officially instituted in the United States in 1982 with the formation of the Society for Disability Studies (Connor et al. 2008; Smith et al. 2009). Understanding that schools must reflect the larger culture, scholars in the field define inclusive education as full participation in general education classrooms with minimal or no segregation into special education services (Connor et al. 2008). They urge that disability be recognized and valued as a natural part of human diversity, that its culture and identity be a part of multicultural curriculums, and that deficit models be rejected (Smith et al. 2009). Unfortunately, disability studies and disability justice initiatives have not managed to significantly undo the negative and hegemonic impacts of WSCP or empiricism on education, special education, or the laws that regulate it. Every student with a learning disability continues to live under the tyranny of an ableist, shallow, and limiting diagnostic system. It is up to teachers and other stakeholders to do the work of shifting our view from a medical pathological illness model toward a relational social injury model so that we can begin to better see students contextualized in their cultural history, their family background, their parenting or lack thereof, their economic formations, their experiences of trauma, etc. In other words, our understanding of the actual child, not the theoretical description of their diagnosis, is what must lead our approach.

A few days after the school meeting for Imani, I got an email from her teacher, Cherylynn. She wanted to meet. I arrived in Cherylynn's science lab classroom, impressed by the resources and equipment. She greeted me warmly, with a bright smile, and invited me to sit. After some small talk, though, I watched as her smile began to dissipate and her demeanor change. "I'm honestly a little embarrassed," she said, "I feel like I've failed Imani." She went on to explain that teaching at a school like this, she and the other teachers would never think that a student might not have a quiet space in their home. There was such wealth at the school that it was hard to imagine any student not having the resources they needed. Cherylynn shared with me that she had been a scholarship student at the same school and that she felt guilty because her experiences then and her experiences now as a young Black teacher navigating a very white wealthy space should have helped her understand Imani better. "I knew there was more there," she said, "but the learning specialist kept saying it was the inattentive ADHD, so I left it at that. I should have listened to my intuition."

I'm willing to bet that Cherylynn's example is not a unique one among teachers. All of us at some point in our careers have quieted or ignored our inner knowing, our intuition about our students, because of the power of science and so-called expertise. And while it was not the case at Imani's school, in many schools the strong divides between regular classroom teachers and special education teachers also encourage such hierarchies. Having a diagnosis often signals to regular classroom teachers that whatever is going on with a student is beyond their expertise and will be addressed by the "specialists" at the school. This approach, as both Imani's and Cherylynn's experiences show, often results in the "othering" of both students and teachers. The fact is, regular classroom teachers are perfectly capable of understanding and unpacking learning diagnoses (with the proper training of course, which should be the real job of the specialists), but when we make these issues the domain of some and not all, we immediately create noninclusivity.

EXAMINING CONTEXT

What does it mean to contextualize diagnosis and to push for methodologies that are not diagnostic but relational? How would this have looked in Imani's case? Although I've often had to use diagnoses like Imani's to advocate against punitive responses to behaviors like sleeping in class, in her case I needed her teachers to engage differently, because the issue wasn't clinical, it was contextual. This shows, I think, the importance of getting to know each student and each story.

I share Imani's story because I felt her school had every resource we usually say we need to do right by every student. They had time, they had money, they had a willingness to learn and do professional development. But the culture of the school, much like Elijah's school, was still WSCP, and the blueprint was empirical data and diagnosis. While a team of eleven people coming together to discuss a child might seem like a dream come true, how does that actually help if none of those eleven people are taking the time to get to know her or are too intimidated to? What if instead of letting the neuropsychological report lead us, we had led with questions like:

Who is this student?

How do they learn?

What works for them and what doesn't?

What's going on in their life?

What do they truly need right now to realign
with the natural state of learning?

A big part of those answers should be coming from the student themself. In short, what if we didn't just talk about centering students without *actually* centering them?

This is why examining things at all these levels is so important. While it is not within our ability to change meetings about students to meetings about ourselves and our systems, we can make shifts in our thinking that can help us be more effective for students within the confines of the systems we have. It's hard to give explicit steps and frameworks in critical approaches because things don't happen in clear steps and often the awareness *is* itself the tool. But if I had a magic wand that I could wave over every school to get them to change their methodology, I would have it make them (1) stop seeing the diagnosis as doctrine, (2) recognize that all healing and hurting happens in relationships, and (3) understand that it is our job and our ethical responsibility to take small actions against the injustices of our system for every student.

Diagnosis Is Not Doctrine

As teachers, we must dethrone the diagnosis and see it as merely a description of the symptoms—not the cause of the student's struggles. ADHD, for example, is a label that describes a set of symptoms such as difficulty sitting still or sitting up; it does not explain other, sometimes deeper reasons for the student's struggles, like personal challenges, learning environment, or unmet emotional needs. Moreover, every tool, from the *DSM*-5 to IDEA to any other used to label and categorize children in the West, has a long and troublesome history behind it and needs to be contextualized. Just as we must see students in the context of their environment—their history, their culture, their experiences—we must take the same approach with our diagnostic tools.

This, according to Freire, is also the first step toward *conscientização*: becoming conscious of the world and the systems we live in. This is especially difficult when the systems you live in actively work to stop you from becoming conscious of them. When I immigrated to the United States at ten years old, I was shocked to find that I had a far deeper understanding of the world, from geography, to sociopolitical relationships, to America's economic ideologies and history, than any adult American I would meet, including my history teachers. This was because I had lived the consequences of America's foreign policy. It is also because I came from a culture that had historically needed to be hyperaware of such issues in order to survive. But to succeed in the US, my deeper knowledge and understanding was actually a hindrance. I wasn't a "deep thinker"; rather, I was labeled an "overthinker," even by educators. This description clearly showed that thinking deeply and critically and questioning the status quo were not valued in American culture, or schooling, but I internalized it as "there is something wrong with me."

Like many educators, I was shocked when a while back I learned that the correlation between ADHD and "justice sensitivity" is being considered as an addition to the list of ADHD criteria in the *DSM*, implying that a heightened sensitivity to injustice is a deficit that can create challenges in life. This is a perfect example of how our methodologies mixed with our WSCP ideologies harm rather than heal. To pathologize the desire to want to fight for justice is the epitome of the absurdity of Western scientific thinking. A methodology that reduces a deeply human and empathetic response as a flaw, instead of recognizing it as a strength that can drive positive change and human growth cannot be trusted.

Still, despite such developments, one could argue that our collective consciousness around the systems that govern us has grown immensely (though not without resistance) over the last few years. The murder of George Floyd, a cataclysmic event that caused waves in the world of education; the COVID pandemic, which caused hidden inequities in our systems to bubble up; and the genocide in Gaza coupled with the fascist response to it on university campuses have all forced us to reflect and question our systems. These events mobilized many students and educators to question race relations, the way American history is taught, our foreign policy, and ultimately our true values as a nation. All this has meant that as educators we are now more aware of the systems that govern us and more willing to question them. But how do we do this in the context of our daily work? Some good questions to ask yourself every time you come to a tension about how a student is doing in your class include:

> Who set the curriculum and the standards this child needs to follow?
>
> Who wrote the rules and the laws by which this child is being governed?
>
> Was this child's voice and the voices of others like them centered?

The answer to these questions will always help you to ensure you are advocating for the child and not for the system.

Knowing students takes time (time teachers often don't have), but I have always been surprised by how much even the most reluctant students want to be known. The simplest personal questions can let students know we are genuinely interested in them. I've had fascinating and informative discussions with students about how their diagnosis feels physically in their bodies, how getting a diagnosis has felt emotionally and what it has meant for them, and whether they see themselves in the same way or differently than others in the family in terms of their thinking and learning. There is so much exploring and unpacking even of the diagnosis itself that we never do and never encourage students to do because we look at it not as a human experience but as a category and almost a disease, as if it's independent of the child and can be examined on its own. This is one of the tragedies of diagnosis in our system. The diagnosis immediately removes the responsibility of knowing the child because they are already "known." This deprives the child of the only thing that can heal them: a safe and loving relationship with their teacher.

Focus on Your Relationship

Research from the field of psychology has shown that it is the therapeutic relationship that heals more than any modality used by a therapist (Norcross 2011; Horvath et al. 2011). A lot more than what our tests can detect goes into what is happening in children's lives that is hindering their ability to socially interact well, to pay attention well, to learn well, and to be self-regulated. It is ultimately connection that heals the brain.

But relationships are complicated because people, both students and teachers, are complicated, and we live in a system that aims to simplify and essentialize human beings and their relationships. This is why Freire says that the second requirement of *conscientização* is understanding our own history and place within systems, both as individuals and as a collective. A teacher-student relationship is, by definition, a relationship of power. For that relationship to become a space for healing, it requires intentional reflection on the part of the teacher and effort to make space for understanding the self, the student, and the dynamic between them.

Another cultural shock for me when I immigrated to the United States was the way in which everything in America seemed to be defined using a binary scale. Black or white, gay or straight, able-bodied or disabled, successful or failed. There was no nuance to anything, nor was there any clear conversation about the power differential between the labels (though it was clear there was one) as the labels always felt more important than what they actually contained.

In her now famous TED Talk "The Danger of a Single Story," Chimamanda Ngozi Adichie unpacks how seeing the world in these simple, non-nuanced ways is actually a byproduct of white supremacy (Adichie 2009). She begins her talk by introducing herself as a storyteller and talks about how as a young child she wrote stories about blue-eyed characters who ate apples and drank ginger beer and played in the snow. She wrote these stories about things she had never experienced because they were what she had read about in the books she had access to as a child. This reminds us not just of how impressionable and vulnerable we are in the face of a story (especially one we are being told about ourselves) but also of how simplistic Western thought has become. White supremacy discourages nuance because there is great power in nuance. If we reduce being human to being white, it's a lot easier for whiteness to stay in power.

This is what Freire means when he says we must understand ourselves as individuals and as a collective. This is what Sylvia Duckworth (2020) encourages us to do in our work around intersectionality and our layered and complex position and relationship to power. This is also what Adichie means when she encourages us to think of ourselves as storytellers. Good storytellers look for nuance and refinements. They get to know their subject. They try to see, create, and present three-dimensional characters who can surprise you, knowing full well the power they hold. Nuance is at the heart of being human and it is at the heart of relationships, but we live in a culture that sees nuance as weak, as messy, and as disorganized. As teachers we have to resist this and instead welcome these tensions.

We also have to realize that to combat the culture and to insist on relationships, with all their messiness, we have to face our own fears and monsters. It is important for all of us, as teachers, to interrogate our own stories first. Understanding ourselves so that we can build relationships isn't just about understanding the differences people with labels like Black or white have—it's actually about recognizing and healing our own traumas around those labels so that we can be in relationship together.

When we give children labels, we are telling their story. We are building it *for* them. This is not to say diagnosis is inherently bad. Disability advocates teach us that naming and owning and being proud of our disability is essential to our identity. But as Adichie explains, we must also be aware of the important role power plays in stories. Who is in power determines whose story is being told, how it is being told, and what is and what isn't being told. But our job is to build tender, vulnerable spaces with children so that we can help them weave their own story. When we test, diagnose, and grade children from our positions of power, we are determining what is being told about them and how. I think about this every time I read a neuropsychology report. Every report tells a story. But no matter how well trained, how culturally competent, how socially and emotionally educated the assessor, the story is being told by someone in a position of power over the one whose story is being told.

Take Small Actions Against Injustice

As previously mentioned, it has been said about antiracist work that racism is not a shark in the water that we must watch out for, it *is* the water (Myhre 2017). The same is true about ableism. We must therefore understand the water we swim in and recognize our own individual and collective positionalities in that water so that we can build compassionate relationships with other swimmers. We must also remember that we can work to filter the water. This is the third step toward *conscientização*: taking action for justice.

Many children in the US live under far more strain than Imani and do not have their basic needs like sleep and hunger met. But the sometimes astounding challenges that students face in their lives (and this is true for students at all socioeconomic levels) are seldom included in our formal testing, questioning, and reporting. Challenging what we read about students, or reading critically (as we encourage them to do), is a small but important way to create change.

We do not need to dismantle and rebuild the entire system at once (although that would be nice) to allow differently abled kids to function. When we recognize the injustices in the system, prioritize the needs of the student over the integrity of the curriculum, and are willing to remain flexible and responsive to how our students show up and what they need, often small changes make big differences for the kids and in the systems. And small changes and tiny battles slowly bring us to bigger ones.

A profound shift happens—for the child, the parent, and the teacher—when we stop treating diagnosis as a fixed label of what is wrong and start seeing it as a lens for understanding. A diagnosis should be a compass, not a cage, useful only when it helps a student name their experience, reclaim their story, move toward healing. When we use diagnoses as guides rather than identities, we resist the deficit-based logic of WSCP that pathologizes difference and move closer to a vision of education rooted in liberation, dignity, and collective care.

CHAPTER 5

COMMUNIZED CARE

Madison was already a junior in high school by the time I met her. She had been diagnosed with ADHD and a mood disorder at age eight and had spent almost a decade on medications for ADHD, depression, and anxiety with little result. Eager to have their very capable daughter attend a school that would positively affect her future career goals, Madison's parents enrolled her in a prestigious college preparatory school without mentioning her diagnoses. Their reasoning was not to Madison's benefit, but it made sense to me. "Madison is a phenomenal singer," her dad told me when we first met, "we wanted her to go to this school because they have a great music program." "And her sister went there and she did so well," her mother chimed in anxiously. "Things were different when we first enrolled her. They didn't have a learning specialist like they do now, and we didn't want her to miss her chance at getting in. And it's a very structured school and we had been told that works well for kids with ADHD." While I could sense, from the moment I walked into their living room, that Madison didn't feel like her parents understood her and perhaps even mistrusted the words they kept repeating, "We just want the best for her," I believed them. As two high-powered attorneys who understood the pipeline to success within the dominant structures, they were worried that Madison could miss opportunities and not meet her potential. Unfortunately, their attempts at helping her were only making things worse.

Madison's freshman year had been challenging, but she had pushed—they all had—and she had gotten through. By the next year, though, under the increasing academic demands of the school along with what her mom described as "social shortcomings" in her peer groups, she had completely crashed. She had failed almost every class and ultimately had to withdraw from the school due to the strain on her mental health. The school, which had itself evolved in response to the changing culture around neurodiversity, had suggested Madison be tested and had proposed a learning skills class if the testing qualified her. Her new testing, done with a psychologist whom I trusted, had affirmed both her diagnoses. But the fact that she had been on medication for so long with no change concerned me. I was also concerned that she had been seeing a therapist for approximately the same amount of time with little change in the mood issues that had led to her crash.

"We've hired every tutor you can imagine. She has a tutor for every subject," her mom continued. "She even saw two educational therapists, but none of it has helped. Nothing has helped, and we just can't have a repeat of last year."

Madison had a commanding presence. She was effortlessly composed and carried the polished ease of someone who seemed to meet every cultural expectation of high school student royalty. With her glowing skin, glossy hair, and warm smile, she looked as if she could have stepped out of a high school TV drama, and all I could think was how surreal it was that someone who seemed to fit the mold so perfectly could still crash so completely. It was as if, no matter how many boxes she checked, one wrong move—one slip in navigating the unspoken rules—could unravel everything, leading to almost brutal judgment and rejection by friends, by the school, and ultimately of course, by herself.

"The problem," Madison's father had also pleaded with me, "is that she can do it, she is smart. If she just wasn't a studious person we would accept that. We would find other ways to encourage her, like singing. But she can get really good grades. She is one of the best writers at her school. She gets A's on essays all the time, and that is not easy to do at that school. But she just can't hold it together."

In my years of work with students, their inability to "hold it together" has always been one of my favorite things about them. I was always so good at holding it together. I still am. That is what the culture demands of us. When I would watch Madison struggling to mask and appear normal, I could understand why her parents were pushing her. She was so close to being able to hold it all together. But then the "lack of regulation" that was described in both her ADHD diagnosis and her mood disorder would kick in, and all the ways she was falling apart on the inside, like all of us, would ooze out and betray her. Her parents told me of huge emotional explosions with nonstop crying followed by days of complete shutdown and an inability to get out of bed. It seemed to me that we should put our attention on what these crashes were communicating, but this was both social and academic suicide in a setting like this school. The last thing anyone there wanted to see was whatever was going on inside. So Madison had to put her focus on the aftermath of it all at school, instead of what was going on with her. She was so close to the perfect package. Why couldn't she keep everything nicely packaged? She seemed just as genuinely curious and concerned about this issue as everyone else in her life.

From our methodologies and frameworks (like the *DSM*-5 and IDEA) grow our actual practice—our treatments, our approaches, our modalities and methods. For too many of us in special education and educational therapy, our approach is to explicitly teach children how to disconnect from themselves and the needs of their minds and bodies and to learn how to mask. In this way, how well a person can pretend and how well they can conform to narrow expectations and definitions of "normal" and "healthy" are what we have come to call mental health. Psychiatric drugs, even programs that aim to help people contain their anger, their outbursts, their defiance, as well as their sadness, depression, and hopelessness—many of which are actually very healthy reactions to their surroundings and circumstances—are often prescribed to help the person conform to cultural norms and societal expectations, most of which, in our capitalist culture, are bound to productivity. Again, it is important to realize that at the heart of this are not the child's desires, but ours. We often want the children to *appear* "normal" because that helps us feel more at ease—not because of any meaningful experiential reason for the child.

I do not say this to argue that psychology and special education have nothing to offer or that we should throw out the baby with the bathwater. Even treatments like cognitive behavior therapy or other behavior-based approaches that I often find difficult to stomach can be of use in certain circumstances. As the Paracelsus saying goes, "All things are poison, and nothing is without poison; only the dose permits something not to be poisonous." We have to critically examine our methods in order to make sure they do not become poisonous. Without taking the time to interrogate, we are always at risk of doing more harm than good in our attempts at teaching and healing. In our attempts at teaching critical thinking, for example, many of us are actually modeling how to not engage critically and to instead continue to uphold the status quo rather than actually listen to and hear our students in order to help them heal within the community. But as part of the neurodiversity revolution we see, teachers and therapists are beginning to shift toward more neurodiversity-affirming approaches that aim to center the student's needs over the needs of the system. In this chapter, I call for you to adopt this approach as well.

ASSESSING ASSESSMENTS

While the issue of our treatment methods being harmful is not limited to students with learning disabilities, it is often these kids, kids like Madison, whom we cannot always successfully shape under our methods, who end up bringing our attention to the harm they can cause. Kids with learning disabilities are often the canaries in the coal mines. To understand the culture of school (especially the culture of inclusion) it's their feelings and experiences that tell us what we need to know. In assessing the efficacy of the methods of a curriculum, they are again the ones who give us the most pertinent information. Yet we ignore their contributions and warnings and instead continue routinely "treating" all students with factory-based definitions of time and space while cutting art and play and literature and teaching inaccurate but self-serving stories and histories, and most notably, specifically teaching students how to limit their thinking to the ideology of WSCP.

Avoiding Reductive Thinking

One common way we do this is by creating multiple-choice tests and then teaching to those tests. This is one of the most efficient ways to cut critical-thinking capacity, to train people to the illusion of forced choice, and in doing so to quash all imagination and creativity. Think of the number of years we spend on this training. Think of how perfectly and how diligently we do it. And then ask yourself whether it could be that, despite all the rhetoric about how the American education system is broken, it is in fact so intentionally well designed and perfectly functioning that we do not even realize that how we define "critical thinking" is itself training for WSCP.

The first time I truly understood this idea of the systems working exactly as they were designed was at a talk by Noam Chomsky. Until then, I had only known Chomsky as a linguist because of my interest in language development in the brain. But in a talk on US foreign policy in West Asia, Chomsky suddenly turned to the role of American education in social control, pointing out how we reinforce conformity and educate out critical thinking through the use of multiple-choice questions in K–12 schooling. By training students to accept a narrow range of previously chosen acceptable answers, he argued, we subtly condition children not only to accept that there is one correct answer, but also that to check off that correct answer, without any room for divergence or independent thought or questioning, is to engage in a meaningful way. What many children with learning disabilities tend to struggle with, however, is an inability to conform to this limited thinking. What is described as neurodiverse—as much as I hate the term—is often used in juxtaposition to what is described as neurotypical. But neurotypical is not the "typical" way that most brains work or are supposed to work. There is no such concept. Every brain is different, and all brains are the same. To me, neurodiversity isn't about thinking or learning differently. We are all meant to learn and think differently. Rather, being neurodiverse is about not being able to force yourself into thinking and learning in the one rigid way that is allowed. In this way, so-called neurodiverse or neurodivergent kids or "learning disabled" kids shine a light not on their limitations but on the limitations of our culture. When advocates call for the centering of disabled voices, it is not just for their sake, but for all our sakes.

As previously mentioned, at the very center of American pedagogy is the written essay. Whether in the K–12 setting or college, the essay is considered the most effective way a person can show their intellect, their creativity, their knowledge of subject. It is by our consideration the antithesis to multiple-choice teaching and testing (which, Madison's parents wanted me to know, is a struggle for her) and the pinnacle of the importance placed by Americans on self-expression (this, they were proud, was not a struggle). But while essay writing is considered a move away from the banking model of education that we often claim is the problem with exams and other forms of assessment, I'm not sure I could say that the perfectly formed essays Madison could write and get A's on, revealed anything meaningful about who she was or what she longed for in her relationships with others. For decades, the argument in progressive education circles has been to value the personal statement or essay over tests like the SAT in college admissions, and learning how to write a well-crafted five-paragraph essay, especially one that can form and defend a thesis, has been the cornerstone and goal of high school curricula, pedagogy, and teaching methods.

At his talk, Chomsky said that while substituting essays for simple multiple-choice tests may appear to engage students in critical thinking, in reality, by offering students a point to debate, we are really teaching them a form of "controlled opposition" and the illusion of choice within a constrained and controlled arena. Moreover, the structure of a five-paragraph essay with a thesis and "evidence" actually reinforces conventional thinking and debate rather than encourages students to challenge dominant ideas and explore alternative visions. Most essay prompts are framed to direct students toward one of a few predetermined positions or interpretations, and they are graded on how well they can conform to a standardized structure and logical coherence. The tools we use to teach critical thinking actually promote splitting complex concepts into binaries and pitting students against an imaginary judge who requires them to make their argument for why they, in fact, hold the only truth using a very specific set of rules about what is considered valid thought, valid evidence, and valid language. Ultimately the student produces a valid false mask of a self and a voice.

The college essay, for example, has always favored rich white cis men. As a brown immigrant woman, I remember being petrified at the idea of my entire academic and professional career riding on a personal essay that required a level of epistemic authority, and privileged personal voice, I simply did not have—not to mention the language barrier. The same is true for many of my neurodiverse students, who become paralyzed at the idea of this personal and creative task not because they are not creative or capable of vulnerability, but because an essay can be a restrictive place for their creative abilities. In addition, their ability to be open and to disclose their differences and needs can gatekeep them from access to college. In other words, those who get ahead in our society are the ones who can present themselves as intellectually superior using very classist, colonial, and WSCP definitions of both intellect and superiority.

Debate Versus Discussion

The fact is, our schooling values debate over true discussion (Figure 5.1). In a discussion, all parties share their perspective. Proposing new ideas is welcomed and even encouraged. The goal is to learn from each other so that by the end, everyone has moved closer to each other. This is very different from a debate, in which opposing arguments are put forth in a formalized, specific way using particular rules. The understanding is that one argument will be made over another and at the end a decision carried. There is no thinking together, no group process, just one individual making points, as if stating a point will make it true. Similarly, there is no

DEBATE VERSUS DISCUSSION

	Debate	Discussion
Definition	A formal argumentative discussion on a particular topic, usually with opposing viewpoints.	An informal conversation or exchange of ideas on a particular topic, often with the goal of reaching a consensus.
Structure	Structured with specific rules, including time limits, turns, and rebuttals.	Less structured, allowing for free-flowing conversation and exploration of ideas.
Tone	Can be more confrontational and competitive. Emotions can be heightened, as participants aim to convince and challenge each other.	Generally more cooperative and collaborative. Emotions are usually more subdued, with a focus on respectful dialogue.
Goal	To persuade the audience and prove one's viewpoint as superior.	To understand different perspectives, share information, and reach a common understanding.
Outcome	One side wins, one side loses.	Shedding misconceptions, developing deeper understanding of a concept.

FIGURE 5.1

understanding that each debater's point of view is going to be colored by their unique lens. Whoever makes the "stronger" argument, or the "better" point, takes the cake. How "better" is decided is itself often a reflection of muscle more than understanding or truth or justice. The question is not about finding equitable solutions that work for everybody but about whose argument can win.

For all the essay and debate topics that have been assigned over decades of American education, for all the thousands, millions even, of students who have addressed them, can we honestly say that we have gotten closer to some truth or justice? The fact is that truth and justice are far more rhizomatic. They are never contained in one point of view. Deep down we know this. We attempt to accommodate it by teaching students to also present the counterargument, as if creating this duality is somehow teaching empathy by getting students to put themselves in each other's shoes. In reality, it is simply using the same techniques to argue a different point. Students are tasked with making an argument using rationality, logic, and evidence (observable data). As a result, students become skilled in the art of distancing, learning not how to listen and cooperate, but how to outmaneuver. This teaching then becomes less about learning how to hold multiple truths and more about proving one right and the other wrong. In the name of intellectual rigor, we reward domination disguised as dialogue and in doing this we not only force students to let go of what comes naturally to them—connecting to others—we also teach them that what is good, natural, and valuable is decimating the other.

Discussion Protocols

How then do we create a culture of true connection? There are three things I have found to be important when it comes to promoting discussion, community building, and collective problem-solving with students. They may seem simple, but they are usually what we don't have and what we need to be intentional about. They are time, attention, and space.

It is only when we give our time and attention to something and create space for it that it actually happens. In my experience, it is good to be intentional with all three. In my work with parents, I make it a point to give fifty minutes of our hour-long session to students and require the parents to do a check-in for the last ten minutes. This is every time, and I take that time seriously. If a parent is unable to do it, I ask that they make up the time.

When it comes to accessing teachers and other professionals in a child's life, it is not as easy to find the time. Here, I create the space instead.

At the end of any meeting about a student, I create a shared Google Docs™ (or other space) in which I ask teachers and all others involved to do a weekly check-in. Every week or two weeks, every individual involved in the student's care—teachers, aides, counselors, and parents—write a brief reflective entry about how the student is doing. Everything from academics, to social-emotional challenges, to successes, to failures can be written here, and we are able to reply to each other's comments. The Google Doc therefore serves as a living document in which we can communicate, and I make a point to mention it in any subsequent meeting. Interestingly, teachers and others who are not able to keep up with this task (after they have agreed to do so) often become more sympathetic to students struggling to follow their directions. This method doesn't work at every school (many don't allow it) or with every teacher (many truly forget or don't have the time); yet just the attempt seems to somehow remind everyone involved of the importance of communication and our responsibility as members of a community surrounding a student.

Finally, as I am a big believer in allowing room for venting and even professional "gossip," I make it a rule to dedicate time and space for team members (including students) to share frustrations, air grievances, and process emotions around a case. So much conflict is avoided when we allow people to decompress, commiserate, and vent frustrations before diving back into problem-solving. These are just some basic examples of ways to be intentional about giving time, space, and attention to mutual communication and community building.

COMMUNIZED CARE

When I began working with Madison, my first suggestion to her parents was to reconsider her school placement. I had not worked with a student at this school before, but I knew of it. It was considered to be one of the more rigorous schools with a very traditional curriculum. They had never been a school to admit kids with learning disabilities, citing simply that they were "not prepared to support them." But with so many students getting diagnosed (some necessary, some not) and so many parents pushing for accommodations like extra time, the school now accepted students with "mild" learning disabilities and referred them out for testing when necessary. "We do not allow for any modifications to our curriculum," I had been advised by the dean of students in my meeting about Madison, "and we do not offer any modifications beyond extra time and a separate testing area." I had been advised about the "study skills" class as a support for "students like Madison" but had also been told that I was not allowed to directly communicate with any of her teachers as "that is not the way we do things here." If Madison was not able to keep up with the demands of the school, "perhaps this is not the right place for her."

As a learning rights advocate, I am very aware of the fact that often what is expected of me is to engage in a debate war and win that debate on behalf of my student. The meetings I attend about students are seldom a community of educators, parents, and other professionals coming together to discuss and arrive at workable solutions for a student though mutual effort and respect. Instead, the very form of the meeting is contentious because in our educational setup it is always a student's job to prove they are worthy of being part of a school community and a school's job to judge whether they have proven that or not. This is especially evident for kids with learning disabilities. The US Constitution does not establish education as a fundamental right. All the laws pertaining to students with disabilities are written such that the only responsibility a school has is to allow a student "access" to their methods or curriculum. Beyond that, it is the student who must assimilate, mask, and prove themselves. There is no obligation for the school to ensure that students are supported in ways that allow them to meet their full potential. No one belongs to a school community just by virtue of being a member of it. The hidden agenda of every meeting about a student, whether they have a learning disability or not, whether the school is public or private, is always an assessment of their very belonging.

Madison's case was no different. Since I was not being offered any real community by the school, my next step was to seek support from her outside community, namely, her therapist and psychiatrist. I learned that Madison had been seeing a Jungian therapist, which for a child and teen made little sense to me, but Madison's mother trusted the therapist because she had previously seen her herself and had found her to be helpful. (For more discussion of Jungian therapy, see below.) I made the point to call her therapist to learn more. I could tell by her shaky voice on the phone that she felt uncomfortable about the call, though she kept reassuring me that she would do anything to support Madison. I inquired about some of the supports she had offered. I was surprised to learn that in the years and years Madison and the therapist had worked together, Madison's parents had been part of the conversation fewer than a handful of times. When I asked what she knew of Madison's struggles at school, the therapist seemed clueless. She seemed to be working in isolation without any connection to the school, Madison's parents, or even her prescribing psychiatrist. My next call was to the psychiatrist, who could not even remember Madison's case. After a long pause, during which he reread Madison's records and refreshed his memory, he reiterated why he had her on the medications she was on. When I shared that neither seemed to be working, he simply said these were the best evidence-based drugs available.

In short, Madison had an entire "community" of people, yet none of them were providing meaningful care for her. She came from a family that was able to afford all these resources, and yet none of these resources were helping her. In fact, I would argue they had worked to disable her further.

In my own short interactions with Madison, I had found a young woman desperate to appear to be okay,

Jungian therapy, developed by Swiss psychiatrist Carl Jung, is a form of psychology that focuses on exploring the unconscious mind to achieve greater self-awareness and psychological integration. Jungian therapy often involves methods like dream analysis, the exploration of symbols and metaphors, and active imagination, a technique in which clients engage with unconscious material through creative expression (Jung 1961, 1979).

While I like Jungian psychology, I believe its methods are better suited for adults. Children and adolescents are still developing the cognitive and emotional tools needed to engage with that kind of symbolic interpretation and abstract thinking.

to keep up, and to save face. At the same time, in just a few hours of work I had found her to have ironically deep insights into her own struggles, with a mature outlook on her own ability and disability. What existed, it seemed, was a chasm between the real Madison and the mask that so many had helped to uphold for so many years. So while my immediate work with Madison still consisted of helping "get her through," exactly as her mother had requested, I wanted to make sure we supported her more authentically—even within the constraints of her very demanding high school schedule. I incorporated some targeted work on her executive functioning, but I also made space for the parts of her life that often got overlooked: at every session, we made sure to set time aside for conversations about her friendships at school, the fears she had about prom, her hesitations about college, her favorite music and artists. There was no sudden breakthrough, no singular moment of healing, but slowly, she began to feel more grounded. I also made a point to stay in close conversation with Madison's therapist, psychiatrist, teachers, and parents. My intention was to build an actual community of care around her where there was meaningful connection instead of a list of expert names that worked in isolation and had little idea of Madison's day-to-day life. My point here is not to portray myself as some great savior. It's simply to say that when any of us intentionally offer children the time, space, and attention they need, they respond. We start to see growth. We have to trust in that.

Realistic Goal Setting

Despite Madison's progress, her mother continued to be concerned. She was worried that Madison was being enabled, not actually learning enough, and not becoming independent enough. "What will happen when she graduates and doesn't have all these supports?" she wanted to know. I explained that they couldn't have it both ways. For a student in Madison's situation to be successful, they needed to focus on only a few carefully selected goals and, importantly, the goals needed to be achievable. This is an important point to remember when in "survival" situations, which schooling often is for kids, especially for kids with learning disabilities. It is impossible to expect children to develop and grow as they would if under healthy supportive circumstances when they are undergoing trauma. For many students, a school setting, ironically, can be very traumatic. Having to meet goals and standards beyond what you are able to do is traumatizing.

This is why accommodating is not enabling. While some may call supports like extra time to complete assignments cheating, I would argue that this thinking is rooted in WSCP. You cannot take away a person's legs, make them run a race, and then call them cheaters for using crutches. Sometimes it is necessary for academic goals to be set aside in favor of guiding students through the act of "doing school." The work may, in many ways, be counterproductive to content acquisition, but sometimes that is what our community has to do for us. They have to hold us while we survive, even enable us in some ways till we find our footing again.

Mutual Aid

In his book *Mutual Aid: Building Solidarity During This Crisis (and the Next)* (2020), Dean Spade makes an important distinction between the idea of solidarity and the idea of charity (called mutual aid in Figure 5.2). Charity, Spade argues, is a top-down approach that is very one-sided. Resources are given from a position of privilege at the top without addressing the root causes of the problem because the ultimate goals of charity are to (1) enhance the positive feelings of the charitable person and (2) keep them in a position of power that requires the other to remain oppressed. The focus therefore is often on alleviating immediate needs without challenging the structures that produce those needs. Solidarity, on the other hand, is rooted in mutual support, equality, and collective action. The emphasis is on reciprocal relationships with the specific aim to dismantle systems of oppression, not just mitigate their effects. Spade argues that mutual aid, as a form of solidarity, is about shared care and interdependence rather than about creating dependency through charity.

Mainstream ideas of how to support those in need of help, such as students with learning disabilities in a classroom setting, rely on the framework of charity and social services. This top-down approach is directly in line with our hierarchical ideologies, a kind of trickle-down economics in the classroom where those in power decide who gets help, how much, and under what exchanges and conditions. In schools, our unjust systems often promote one

CHARITY VS. MUTUAL AID

	Charity	Mutual Aid
Definition	Voluntary giving of help, typically in the form of money or goods, to those in need	Cooperative assistance and support among individuals or groups, often based on shared needs or goals
Focus	Helping those in need	Building solidarity and community resilience
Structure	Usually organized by institutions or individuals	Often decentralized and grassroots
Reciprocity	Often one-way giving	Based on the principle of reciprocity, mutual support among participants
Longevity	Can be short-term or long-term, depending on funding and resources	Can be sustained over time through ongoing relationships and networks

FIGURE 5.2

type of learner at the expense of others. To make ourselves look and feel better, those in power, in this case neurotypical school leaders (including teachers), create an entire "special" education system to help disabled children fight their way onto our level. It is not hard to see that the system promotes an ableist belief that able-bodied and able-minded people deserve to be on top.

Just as our laws and systems of government (or in the private sector, individual wealthy people) decide who is worthy of charity, in our school system we educators are the gatekeepers who, using a set of eligibility requirements that stem from ableist and racist roots and often work to perpetuate them, determine which student deserves charity. This is how we end up in situations where parents feel pressured to allow a child to fail in order for them to be eligible for support and services in a system that allocates services based on a measure of how far a child falls from an arbitrary norm created by neurotypical and ableist standards. Like public jobs and industries now in place to help "fight homelessness," special education teachers often become little more than "managers" providing "limited and conditional access" to supports.

This view may elicit a lot of feelings for teachers, especially special education teachers, who often see themselves being victimized in unfair systems that don't value them or their work. But that too is a result of our individualistic and top-down ideology. One of the great tricks that capitalism plays on educators, mental health professionals, and others in the healing industry is to sell them the dream of helping and healing. We are taught that if we go to school and get degrees, often at an exorbitant cost, we get to help heal the trauma that the system is creating. But this is a lie because the trauma created by the system will always outweigh the efforts of those working as a filter. This lie is exacerbated by the creation of private charitable industries (like my own field of educational therapy) where we help uphold and legitimize the oppressive school system by "supporting" outside the classroom students . . . who can afford to pay.

In helping us understand how we can resist these notions, which include our own burnout in WSCP systems, bell hooks argues that we must instead embrace a concrete practice of care and respect with intentionality and action (hooks 2000a) where love, including self-love, is practiced in community where we all share responsibility for one another. There is a huge difference, much like the difference between charity and solidarity, between seeing ourselves as offering support to a student whose well-being is their responsibility to a vision where we are responsible for their well-being, as they are for ours. Such a vision of community as a radical practice of solidarity challenges the top-down, expert-driven models of care we currently have, where educators, mental health professionals, and administrators are positioned as "helpers" to "fix" students.

Community organizer and philosopher Grace Lee Boggs offers some insight on what an actual radical, transformative community looks like. She writes, "We can begin by doing small things at the local level, like planting community gardens or looking out for our neighbors. That is how change takes place in living systems, not from above but from within, from many local actions occurring simultaneously" (Boggs 2011, 97). As Boggs teaches, community building is not about the heroic acts of an individual teacher saving their marginalized students in an oppressive system despite all odds. Teaching toward a new vision of care is less about taking on extra work and more about creating spaces for collective growth, where every member of the classroom—whether neurotypical or neurodivergent, privileged or marginalized—has a role in contributing to a new vision of care. It's about fostering an environment where care is shared and mutually reciprocal and rhizomic rather than one-sided, paternalistic, centralized, and top down.

Outside our individualistic tendencies to think one person can make a change, we sometimes like to think that one teacher, one tether, one stable guiding adult can help a child thrive. And there is some research that supports this (Werner and Smith 1992; Scales and Leffert 1999). But for children to truly thrive, we need true community-driven solidarity.

Communities, like individuals, have their own culture, environment, history, and material conditions, and all of these play a role. When thinking about the community around a child we have to ask ourselves these questions: To what extent are the teachers, parents, grandparents, therapists, and peers around a student aware of their needs, challenges, and strengths? Does this student have spaces in a community where they feel connected, seen, and supported? When we don't find these supportive communities, instead of trying to become them for the child by ourselves, we might ask these questions: How can we create more connections, more networks? How can we encourage those already in touch with a student to do the same? How can we advocate for better, more effective, and cohesive communication among members of the communities around a student? How can we actively facilitate the relationships around them and help them do the same? In some cases, we might try to connect a child to new people, spaces, and networks. In other cases, we might try to strengthen already existing connections. The point is to remember that neither we, nor the student, can do it all on our own.

DIALOGUE

What I found most frustrating in my experience with the community surrounding Madison was the intentional silencing of dialogue, which is essential to community building. There is no question that this intentionality was fueled by the white supremacist ideology at the core not just of her school but of most schools and the psychoeducational industrial complex. It is not by accident that there is such little dialogue and communication even between different modalities within, say, psychology, much less between psychology and education and medicine. The compartmentalization of expertise and knowledge has made it so we cannot have the simplest of dialogues. Instead, a paternalistic and assimilative voice rules supreme and it drowns out, monitors, and disallows commonsense dialogue about a student's well-being. But why is this?

Decolonial visionary and teacher Trinh Minh-ha (2009) explains:

> *You who understand the dehumanization of forced removal-relocation-reeducation-redefinition, the humiliation of having to falsify your own reality, your voice—you know. And often cannot say it. You try and keep on trying to unsay it, for if you don't, they will not fail to fill in the blanks on your behalf, and you will be said.* (80)

Dialogue requires an ongoing commitment to be *with* the people. But this lies in direct contradiction to a system that aims not to be with its students but rather to sort and ultimately exploit them in order to offer them at the altar of the system. True dialogue is an emancipatory process that results in the social empowerment of communities. Ultimately, in my conversations with Madison around the struggles she was having with her friends, I came to understand that there, too, there seemed to be a disconnect about the importance of true dialogue in community building. Perhaps because of the modeling at their schools, exacerbated by the new rules of dialogue dictated by social media, many young people today long for connection and community but are not willing to acknowledge that there is a price to be paid for that. Relationships are work and they are messy. They require a willingness to give not just our time and attention, but control. Community requires soft skills, small talk, vulnerability, and the capacity to be embarrassed. When our therapists tell us "we don't owe anyone anything" in the name of mental health or encourage us to cut people off when they cross our boundaries, all while social media connects us to daily dopamine hits without exacting any cost to us, we forget that to reap the benefits of the love and care that comes from relationships and community, we not only have to put in labor for it, we have to be willing to accept some risk. We have to get comfortable with things like the pain of growing social skills, wasting time on small talk, being willing to be wrong, to endure distress, to take responsibility for personal failings, or to have a fallout or a fight. This price may be even higher for kids who struggle with social skills, but ultimately, we all have to work to develop these skills.

Freire's approach to pedagogy (Freire and Macedo 1995) necessitated that we move from "speaking to" to "speaking with" others, which implicitly communicates respect for the knowledge and dignity that others bring to our dialogue. Freire and Macedo (1995) argue:

> *Dialogue characterizes an epistemological relationship. Thus, in this sense dialogue is a way of knowing and should never be viewed as a mere tactic to involve students in a particular task. We have to make this point very clear. I engage in dialogue not necessarily because I like the other person. I engage in dialogue because I recognize the social and not merely the individualistic character of the process of knowing. In this sense, dialogue presents itself as an indispensable component of the process of both learning and knowing. (379)*

To achieve this kind of dialogue between clinicians and teachers and students (and among students themselves) requires meaningful opportunities to engage with one another across our differences. It means earnestly involving communities, families, young children, students, faculty, and all that are directly impacted by the research and the practice. This, of course, requires the humility to let go of the arrogant shield of expertise often found in professionals (or the arrogant shield of popularity among students) and to instead enter these relationships as vulnerable and open human beings. This also will require a commitment to dialogue even when it seems like the difficult choice or too time consuming. In this way, dialogue can become an earnest attempt to engage about others with respect for who they are rather than adhering to a common tendency to see them as who we need them to be.

Communized care, then, requires that we see the whole community as responsible agents in healing. The Canadian education and environmental activist Wendy Priesnitz (2000) argues that "public education reflects our society's paternalistic, hierarchical worldview, which exploits children in the same way it takes the earth's resources for granted" (12). Arguably, teaching and healing methods that begin not with the questions and agency of those who will be impacted by them will always be exploitative. The value of communized care stems from the belief that finally, from this paradigm, the practice of teaching would aim to have specific impact that is meaningful to the place where the work is ongoing. In other words, instead of seeking to be universally valid, research and practice would be rooted in local places, performed to meet the specific needs of the community, and aimed at its long-term survival through practical and applied goals. What does it mean to see and hold all of us parents, teachers, therapists, neighbors, cousins, aunts, friends, politicians, leaders (and the list goes on) accountable for the healing of every member of our community? It means we need to acknowledge that no one individual can create any of these changes—this is a big shift as we often remind teachers and therapists that they alone can create this type of change—instead, all of us are responsible.

The starting point for mutual aid is the shared understanding that the systems we live in—in this case the schools—cannot meet our needs, and we must therefore meet them together. The end point is pressuring the systems and power structures to change, but first we must accept that what we are given in the form of direction, diagnosis, IEP goals, assessments, therapies, etc. are not enough and are not working. We begin with our common sense and our mutuality, we look at what is actually needed for the child, and we try to recruit and then maintain through direct action, cooperation, mutual understanding, and solidarity that which we feel the child needs. In other words, to the extent possible, we work outside the unjust systems of power, realizing that we must depend on each other; most importantly on each other's humanity and empathy over what the structures of power provide for us.

There is a great deal of informality here. And for a field that has largely been pushed to become more formal, more scientific, more professional, more educated, more legitimate in the eyes of science and business, this may seem very counterintuitive. But teaching has always been an informal business. It is in a way the paradox of it—to literally engage in the formation of a mind, a human, a consciousness, a kind of brain surgery, but to do it through the simplest connecting of hearts. That is the work of teaching. This communized care is not just about the group of carers and communities we build around students, it is also about the caring we offer during one-on-one interactions with the child. Communized care is a belief, it is an attitude, that we are in fact all important, looked after, cared for, by the infinite network of life itself. All of science and the most basic common sense proves this. Life itself is proof of communized care. It takes an incredible amount of brainwashing, trickery, and indoctrination to disconnect children from this innate understanding and to convince them they are alone. It takes profound severing and trauma to do this. Our job as teachers, as healers, is to welcome children back to that connection.

CHAPTER 6

A NEW VISION

When I first started college at the University of Pittsburgh, I was surprised and dismayed by the actual physical distance between some of my classes. In high school, I had already felt this separation and compartmentalization of knowledge, with many department heads and teachers never showing much interest in engaging with other department heads or teachers despite seeing them daily. Even something as simple as coordinating calendars so we as students didn't end up with three tests on one day seemed out of reach. I couldn't understand how so many seemingly simple tasks were impossible, while something as unnatural as segregating knowledge, which it seemed could only be done through deliberate division and intentional wall building, was so perfectly achieved.

In my naiveté, I had hoped that things would be different in college. Surely in a university setting there would be an insistence on dialogue and the exchange of ideas, of scientific, philosophic, artistic, and even spiritual discourse; of ways of seeing the world and constructing it anew. Universities were where people went for "higher" education.

My disappointment was overwhelming.

Since my family did not have the resources to take me on any college visits, when I first arrived on campus the sheer vastness of the space was a shock. Endless lawns; old, beautiful buildings; a campus covering so many blocks we would sometimes take the city bus to get from class to class. But all that space, which at first embodied the expansion I had hoped for in my mind and heart at university, quickly began to become an instrument of constriction. By the time the green lawns were covered in winter snow, I knew that each of the ornate gothic buildings that housed different departments was separated from the others by something far thicker than stone walls and long pathways. The city bus that I had been so excited to ride for "free" as a college student soon became a symbol not of connection and dialogue between disciplines but rather of the insurmountable distance between different fields. Knowledge wasn't just disconnected, it was at war with itself, with department heads competing for everything from recognition to resources. But worst of all, nobody seemed to question any of this. Not faculty, not students, no one. In the end, this lack of reflection and questioning, in a space that was supposed to have been built for exactly that purpose, became harder for me to endure than the Pittsburgh winters.

Like so many "smart" immigrant kids from chaotic families, school had always been a lifeboat for me. Accepting that the lifeboat itself was just another system designed to maintain its own structure crushed the very tether that had kept me afloat for years. I didn't want to understand learning or teaching anymore. I didn't want to figure out and untangle how we could make schools better. I felt deceived by a propaganda machine more sophisticated than anything the Islamic Republic could have been accused of creating. I wanted nothing to do with the lie of education. After graduating, I spent a year of couch surfing at my younger brother's apartment in an utter state of confusion about how to move forward in the world.

This is how the kids I work with today saved me. I took a job just to appease my brother, who was slowly growing impatient with my inertia. The first time I sat across from a student I was told had a "learning disability," I knew I had been wrong to fret. Like me, they were disillusioned by a system that seemed to have everything as its goal except meeting the basic, naturally occurring human needs of its students, all the while proclaiming its commitment to democracy, humanity, and child-centeredness. And from that first moment, and in every moment after, I understood that what these students needed from me most were not my skills or credentials but rather the deep sense of knowing that connected me to them.

"To engage in dialogue," hooks writes, "is one of the simplest ways we can begin as teachers, scholars, and critical thinkers to cross boundaries, the barriers that may or may not be erected by race, gender, class, professional standing, and a host of other differences" (hooks 1994, 130). This is how my students heal me and I them. In dialogue, we move beyond the roles assigned to us—teacher, student, "abled," "disabled"—and into a space of mutual recognition, beyond the labels and assumptions that divide us. In this small space, this fifty-minute exchange across a table, we reclaim what hooks so aptly calls radical love. My students taught me, one session at a time, that connection and dialogue, truly listening to understand, being vulnerable and raw are how you break down the barriers we have erected and, in the process, reclaim not only knowledge but ourselves.

A NEW VISION: RADICAL LOVE

We have an incredibly limited understanding of love in our culture. James Baldwin speaks of this directly when he contrasts meaningful, more mature notions of love with the shallow version we are allowed in American culture when he compares "the tough and universal sense of quest and daring and growth" to "the infantile American sense of being made happy" (Baldwin 1962). Other cultures, even the Greeks, recognize love in many forms—not just romantic or sexual, but communal, philosophical, and ethical. Love, in its fullest sense, requires commitment, embracing the unknown, even pain. This kind of love is the foundation of true community, a foundation that is increasingly rare in modern life. For many of us today, school is the one remaining communal space, and many of us struggle as we are forced to replace it as we get older with a workplace that often tries to pretend to be a community but is anything but. How do we protect one of our few remaining communal spaces? My aim is to invite you to make your classroom into a community of resistance, fueled by radical love and an ethic where the highest love is the love for hope.

Inherent in radical love is radical acceptance. We don't usually think of these concepts as related to mental health, but a sign of mental health is the extent to which we have been able to acknowledge, accept, and integrate all parts of ourselves. As so-called neurodivergent people repeatedly say, what is most disabling, most shaming, is the pathologization, the othering, and ultimately the rejection of their ways of thinking and functioning that does not match the dominant way. How could a field that claims to be about healing, whether psychology or education, be primarily based on categorizing for the purpose of othering and rejecting instead of loving and accepting? As important as diagnosis can be, I spend more time helping children (and parents) manage their relationship to the diagnosis, navigating shame around something that should be setting them free and helping them feel more understood instead of more ashamed. A diagnosis is only as good as it helps us accept and integrate parts of ourselves.

Lately, I have noticed a trend where at the beginning of an IEP meeting, everyone is asked to go around and say something positive about or an area of strength of the student. This is not a bad practice per se, but I do find that it's a surface-level way of understanding why we must shift from a deficit-focused perspective to one that celebrates differences. Instead of starting with a list of strengths like "she is kind" or "he does really well socially" or "they are respectful," we must dig deeper and share what we actually know about a student. This is also a great reminder to get to know our students. Many teachers think preparing for an IEP meeting means reading the student's testing, but what I would prefer is to hear an anecdote, or a personal encounter, good or bad, that speaks to something a teacher truly saw, not something they assumed, read, or prepared. Speaking to something authentic and real, however small, humanizes students and automatically shifts us from a deficit-based model.

For your struggling students especially, this is my plea to you. See if you can sit with them for just a few authentic minutes at a time. It might take months of trying before you get a real minute, but trust that minute more than you trust anything you are told about that child or anything that is written about them. Children want to reveal themselves to us. They long for it, not just because they need our help and our guidance, but because that's what each of us comes to this planet to do. We come to change the world not by seeing and healing it, but by seeing and healing ourselves. What a privilege it is to help someone else do that, to help hold the light for them so that they know their journey matters.

Radical Empathy

One of the great byproducts of the current culture wars we find ourselves in, specifically around education and teaching, is that so much of what has always been an implicit part of the culture is suddenly now being explicitly spoken. While we may want to disregard groups like Moms for Liberty, for example, as fringe, it is important that we realize they are giving voice to deeply held beliefs about fundamental concepts around schooling and parenting in America. When we hear them explicitly say that they don't want their children to learn empathy, or that "not every human is deserving of my child's empathy," we need to look beyond just the fights over the programs they are opposing and think about what this says about our culture. The tendency is to disregard these voices as unbelievable or sociopathic, but the fact is, this has been the culture and the goal all along. It is not a coincidence that billionaires in our government today refer to empathy as a "civilizational bug" (Wong 2025). You cannot kill and take land and then enslave and build a country if you have empathy. Lack of empathy is a cornerstone of American success and exceptionalism. In this way, Moms for Liberty or Elon Musk are actually quite right. They are earnestly sounding the alarm that if we begin to cultivate empathy, if we begin to humanize the other, if we let go of our sociopathy and become human ourselves, we will lose the country as we know it. This is not just a legitimate concern but an absolute truth.

I have watched as children's faces have shifted to disbelief when they hear me agree with their version of the story, their point of view, their "complaint" and "defiance" for which they are usually labeled everything from lazy and sassy to insubordinate and mentally ill. I have watched some burst into tears. No one can know the stories children tell themselves, the conclusions they make about their own part in the dysfunction around them, until you say one true thing like "It's okay that you can't read that" and you watch a child become unglued and put their head on your shoulder, a practical stranger, and cry, sobbing as they realize that maybe it is okay, maybe I am okay, maybe I'm not bad because I don't know how to read, maybe I'm not dumb, maybe I'm not the reason my parents fight or my teacher is frustrated and the million other things they connect their own "badness" to even without an adult suggesting it. In that moment, the act of listening to their story, of sitting with them quietly as they cry, shifts the very core of their being. This is where empathy is not a passive feeling but an active practice.

In the classroom setting, radical empathy means creating an entire classroom culture in which both students and teachers can feel safe to share their experiences, to be heard, and to listen. This can only happen when we model what it looks like to acknowledge feelings and accept challenges. Today, in the name of empathy, we sometimes confuse understanding with excusing. This doesn't mean that we expect less of our students or excuse harmful behavior or avoid accountability. True empathy doesn't lower expectations; in fact, it requires that we hold them accountable as responsible members of the community we are building together.

Radical empathy, therefore, must be collective, and it must also be active. It is not enough to cultivate empathy as individuals. hooks' famous admonition that "love is an action, never simply a feeling" (2000a) is a call to action to build networks of support that transcend our own lives and even our classrooms and schools. If groups of educators can come together to learn how best to teach math, so too can we come together to uplift one another and push back against systems that are indifferent to our collective well-being.

Embracing radical empathy is not just about teaching our students to be better, more compassionate people, nor about trying to do that in our own personal or professional lives. Rather, the call is to push back against a culture of dehumanization that has long been at the core of American success and cross over to a way of being that values connection over control and humanity over hierarchy.

Radical Self-Care

What I sometimes hear when I do work with teachers is, "But you have the luxury of time and one-on-one work. How can you expect us to do this with thirty kids in a class?" It's a valid point. When a system is set up for profit so that the goal is to see the highest number of kids one adult can manage, the kind of attention and attunement required in education goes out the window. It is unfortunate that because of our systems, the time we do spend on a student (for example, in an IEP meeting, in a one-on-one resource setting, or conferring with a student in the classroom) is often spent on the system and not the student. I have been in IEP meetings, for example, where we have spent more time on the language of a goal that is ultimately meaningless for the student or talking about a child's struggles than we do actually seeing them. When I report on what actually happens for a student during a task, many teachers suddenly have incredibly innovative alternatives or ways to support the student. But it takes willingness to transgress the lines of how these meetings are structured and a push for almost an informality in the conversation that allows them to access their creativity. In other words, teachers are bound and exhausted by the same oppressive structures as students. And these "professional" boundaries can get in the way of teaching by promoting disengagement and a lack of true dialogue and praxis. I feel my students letting out a sigh of relief, as if stepping out of a rigid cast, when I dismantle the rules by which they must abide. And I watch teachers do the same, allowing themselves to breathe when I ask them to lay down the rules and just talk about the real human child. Suddenly magic happens and we come up with simple but life-changing solutions for that student in the same time frame we would have otherwise been talking legalese.

But the problem is even bigger. In our current systems, if a teacher takes the time after class to explain things to a student, if they allow them to turn in their work late or call home when they are absent, or if they connect them to a counselor for a ten-minute check-in, we think they have met our required standard of care. Similarly, if that teacher takes a "mental health day" when they need it and go to the botanical garden or get a massage, they feel they have engaged in self-care. But radical self-care, as articulated by the Black feminist poet and activist Audre Lorde (1984, 2017) and others, differs fundamentally from these limited approaches to care. The difference is in the aim of the acts of care. In our current mainstream models of care, the aim is to help the individual "recharge" or "manage their stress" so they can come back and engage in the system again. In these models, there is no questioning of the structural forces that produce burnout, inequality, oppression, and mental health challenges. What our current models, including therapy, give us is a list of individual coping mechanisms rather than communized ways to confront the systems that are causing harm in the first place.

Lorde, in her essay "Uses of the Erotic: The Erotic as Power" (1984), urges us to understand care as a collective, transformative force that involves recognizing our shared humanity and acting in solidarity with others rather than retreating into isolation. Radical care, in her framework, is not about learning how best to cope with oppressive systems but to actively resist those systems in ways that uplift everyone in the community.

I hear today the phrase "rest is resistance" without seeing any real evidence of actual engagement in resistance work. Lorde was a fierce and active revolutionary and community activist. Within that context she wrote the now famous words "caring for myself is not self-indulgence, it is self-preservation" (2017, 131). For teachers, embracing true radical love and communized care means stepping away from the conventional "savior" mentality in our profession where we are not only expected to take on the emotional and intellectual labor of saving students from their struggles but to also encourage them to work hard so that they can "make it" in tomorrow's capitalist machine. It means refusing to take our own place in that machinery without pushback. It means building communities of mutual care and aid where students and teachers and parents and therapists sustain each other. Sometimes, simply surviving is the only option, but this is not sustainable over a thirty-year career. Creating a pedagogy and a praxis that genuinely heals and transforms has to be more than about "getting through the day" or "getting through the year." It requires resisting a system that continually extracts labor from educators without regard for their well-being and instead reimagining the role of the teacher and the student and the surrounding community as relational and reciprocal.

As hooks notes, "love is an action, never simply a feeling" (2000a), and it is in the practice of this kind of radical love that we need to begin to transform our methods and our pedagogy into ones of healing and care. When we center radical care in our methods and our pedagogy, we recognize that the aim is not just to care for our students but ourselves. We share of ourselves and the ways in which we are being impacted by external forces of oppression—poverty, racism, sexism, etc.—and understand that even Freud knew that "our cures are cures of love" (Nunberg and Federn 1962).

Building a pedagogy rooted in radical love and shared care starts by shifting how we relate to our students. It starts by seeing them not just as learners but as people alongside us on a path of growth and revolution. It means valuing honest conversations and connection over strict hierarchies. It means seeing students as full human beings, engaged in the same resistance with us and paying attention to their emotional needs and our own and inviting them into dialogue rather than calling them out.

This kind of teaching takes ongoing reflection. It can only happen when we engage with every step, questioning our beliefs, seeing our work as relational and political, and rejecting the idea that education is about individual success or survival; rather, it is about building a community of care that supports the flourishing of all its members. It is about seeing our own role as teachers as prophetic, political, psychological, and spiritual. This is the pedagogy that we must move toward—not just for the sake of our students, but for our own sanity and well-being as educators.

RADICAL LOVE IN ACTION

The turmoil of the past almost decade of American politics has pushed my work even more toward training and working with adults. In addition to my ongoing work with families and students, I spend much of my time helping educators and mental health professionals work their way through my 4C framework. I regularly find myself telling these colleagues, every time a new event puts us in a new panic, that we already have blueprints for what to do, there are already texts and theories and language to help us, we do not have to reinvent the wheel. And I do my best to help bring them to these road maps, to summarize and connect the dots in a way that helps us all walk the path together.

One practice that really helps is participating in small biweekly videoconferences to discuss how the 4 C's (collective ideology, connected experience, contexualized diagnosis, and communized care) intersect with our lives and with the lives of our students. In these groups of no more than twelve people, we create a sacred space—a space where all are welcome to bring whatever is coming up for them. We have weeks where one member talks (and sometimes cries) about something going on in her professional life, weeks where we all engage in an activity that helps further our knowledge and understanding, and weeks where folks might not even show up or show up but keep their camera and audio off. We spend the time to get to know each other, professionally and personally, and when geographically possible (I run one group of only Southern California colleagues), we get together outside our regular time to eat, dance, go to events, visit each other's homes, and hug each other. There is no question that the answer to all our questions and all our problems is community. And I am lucky to be a member of a few very special communities in my life.

I invite you, as teacher leaders, to consider taking a step to create a Radical Love Group in your community. While all our communities are important, having a professional community dedicated to decolonization and centering radical love in our practice will help you meet the challenges of being a teacher, or a healer of any kind, in our violent systems in ways other communities cannot. You may start this at your own school or open it up to your district. You may feel more comfortable doing this with colleagues across the nation. Many of you may already have professional groups or communities. Consider intentionally bringing in this lens and this type of work into that group, if the other members agree. Others of you may find this idea overwhelming and not want to spend even more of your limited time dealing with work colleagues. If that is the case, consider finding existing groups where someone with knowledge is already doing the work of leading and organizing and you can join without a big commitment. Alternatively, start meeting with just one person you like and see how the group grows over time.

If nothing else, I hope you take away from this book that building community, specifically, building community with like-minded people in a semistructured way, is essential to decolonizing work. This is not just part of your self-care, it is an ethical responsibility to yourself and to the profession. We cannot do this work alone, nor can we do it in our heads, purely in theory. We must bring it into our actual lived experience. That's what praxis means in teaching.

In the pages of this book, you have patiently traversed the layers of Western scientific knowledge with me. It is in the image of empirical science that our education system is built, with all its beauty and all its flaws. Ten years into my practice as an educational therapist, I once again found myself disillusioned. Why was the work I was doing with students limited to private sessions outside the classroom? Why were the clear answers of empirical research about how to remediate learning disability not making its way into schools? But most importantly, I was faced with the question of why, after a decade of work advocating for kids, I still felt my work was more about forcing students to assimilate than about changing the systems. I wanted to learn, and to understand at more systemic levels, where things were breaking down. This is what brought me back to school and to my doctoral work. But I was determined not to fall into the old empirical systems again. I would not study clinical psychology or even history and policy for the answers. I knew I needed a different way. This time I would try to learn from those who, like me, saw a system failing on purpose and knew it was their responsibility to critique it. This is what brought me to critical pedagogy.

The goal of this framework (which developed from my doctoral work and my ongoing work with students and schools) is to offer a radical reimagining of the foundational practice of special education, through these interconnected pillars. I want to emphasize that this framework is not a step-by-step set of instructions for you to follow. In fact, my hope is that, after reflecting on some of what you have read in this book, you will move to develop your own framework for teaching for liberation and love. Take these not as a linear set of steps, but an integrated and repeating process of moving yourself and your students in new directions.

This framework rests on the four pillars we have unpacked together (Figure 6.1). In place of the dominant Western ontology rooted in white supremacist, capitalist, patriarchal structures, we begin with a collective ideology—an understanding that being is inherently relational, and every person holds intrinsic value by virtue of their place in the collective whole and their connection to others. We do not have to deny Elijah's disability to affirm his worth, his value is affirmed simply by his existence. From there, in place of an empirical epistemology that sees only detached observation as legitimate and therefore sees our suffering as separate, we center a connected and relational epistemology, one where knowledge emerges through our embodied experiences, authentic connections, and interdependence. Such an epistemology would mean the struggles of kids like Olivia can be seen not as pathologies to be corrected, but as expressions to be understood—where a struggle to turn in work is held with curiosity, care, and recognition and where brilliance is recognized as something that isn't diminished by timing. Similarly, in contrast to traditional methodologies that see diagnosis as doctrine and locate a disease within the brains and bodies of children, a contextualized diagnosis would see the whole of children like Imani, considering all the forces—personal, political, and biological—that can be influencing them. And finally, rather than pedagogical methods designed to sort, rank, and universalize children like Madison, we would advocate for a system of communized care, of local, meaningful, justice-driven approaches to curriculum and healing that support connection, not competition. Rejecting the scientific gold standard of objectivity and unbiased search for knowledge, this social justice paradigm recognizes that all knowledge is ideological, political,

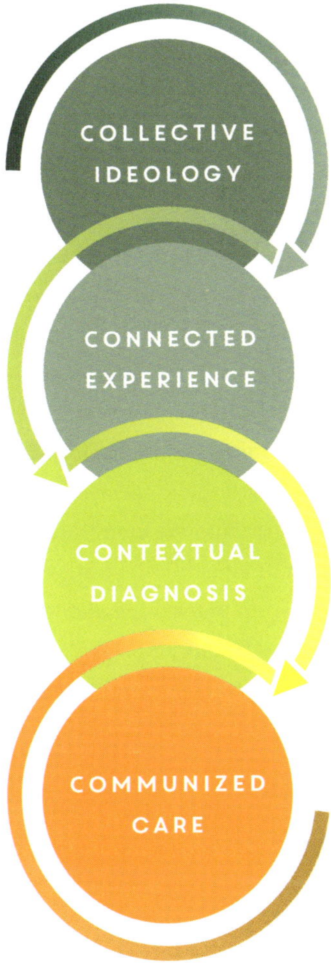

FIGURE 6.1

cultural, historical, and spiritual and encourages a deep understanding and recognition of the interconnectedness and holism of nature, moving beyond boundaries of objective measurement. Nothing I present to you now is new, but I hope that it is revolutionary, as it is my take and my synthesis of the work of the many who have been holding the line against epistemicide and hegemony from the outset.

This framework began to materialize for me during my dissertation work and has since evolved in my work with teachers and therapists as well as students and parents and even in the writing of these pages. I therefore expect it to continue to evolve and change as my own understanding deepens in exchanges with people like you, people at the frontlines of the revolution. The framework, as I imagine it, is a mirror that stands in front of the foundational layers of Western thought, much like my students stood as mirrors to my own thinking and training and doubts within this tradition. It aims to offer both critique and support as we ask the ever-important question in teaching and learning: How else can we understand this? Finally, central in this paradigm, is the ongoing goal of making a specific, grounded impact that is meaningful to the place where the work is happening. In other words, instead of aiming for universal validity, what makes this framework work is how it's rooted and implemented in your local context—your classroom, your clinic, your practice, your school. It's about meeting the needs of your actual community, not an imagined one. Consider this a porous, fluid blueprint that's meant to be adapted, reshaped, and reimagined. The goal is not to replicate, but to evolve your own personal models and practices based on what you notice and need.

Figure 6.2 offers examples I've either implemented myself, seen working in schools and other spaces, or dreamed up alongside students, teachers, and colleagues. Some are still aspirations, others are small changes that made a big difference. Use them as suggestions, not prescriptions. Start with one. Make it your own. Let it grow slowly.

FIGURE 6.2

Living the 4Cs

1. Collective Ideology

a. **See the IEP as a political document.**

In IEP meetings, ask out loud: "Whose standards are these goals based on?" "Whose values are being centered?" "Who benefits from this standard?" "Does this reflect what the student actually wants or needs?" Challenge the idea that grade level always equals success.

b. **Consider positionality during supervision.**

When discussing cases or students, take time to reflect: How is my background shaping how I see this child or family? What assumptions am I making based on how I was raised, trained, or treated in school?

c. **Teach the history of special education.**

Talk with colleagues about how special education didn't appear out of nowhere. It came from families and disabled people fighting for basic rights. Learn about case law. What language did the courts use? Why? Who was the law written to benefit?

d. **Walk the school with new eyes.**

Do a walkthrough of the school with a trusted colleague and ask: "Who is this space built for?" "What are the messages on posters, murals, signs?" "Who feels safe here? Who doesn't?" Or take students or staff on a "critical history walk" of the school or neighborhood (this could even be virtual), naming the history, what's been erased, and the historical formations of this space.

2. Connected Experience

a. **Create agreements with students, not for them.**

Start the year by asking students about dignity, care, rest, and joy. Ask what helps them feel respected, what gets in the way, and how they want to handle conflict. Write those agreements together as part of the classroom rules and revisit them often.

b. **Invite families and elders into staff professional development.**

Host a panel with parents, grandparents, and former students who've received special education services. Ask them what worked, what harmed, and what they wish staff understood. Listen without defensiveness.

c. **Offer group-based support.**

Instead of relying only on one-on-one sessions, offer peer groups where students can talk about what it's like to navigate school while struggling, masking, or being labeled. Create spaces where students don't feel alone—particularly for students from collectivist cultures. Experiment with peer circles and lunch-time storytelling spaces.

d. **Celebrate with music, food, and movement.**

Once a month, hold a classroom or schoolwide celebration. Let students bring in a song they love, share a food that means something to their family, or lead a short dance. Joy should not be a reward—it should be part of the structure. Invite students to keep a photo journal on their phones of things that bring them joy throughout their days and have them share regularly.

3. Contextualized Diagnosis

a. **Add liberation goals to IEPs.**

Audit records and rewrite deficit language. Add goals to IEPs, such as: *Can identify ableist barriers in their school environment. Can explain what helps them focus. Can ask for a break without apology.* Or *Can say when something doesn't feel fair.* These are real skills, not extras.

b. **Track harm, not just grades.**

Push your school or district to conduct equity audits. Look at which kids are being sent out of class, restrained, misdiagnosed, or never referred for services. Keep a simple spreadsheet. Are boys being over-referred? Are girls with challenges dismissed? Are immigrant students' language needs impacting their diagnosis? Bring that data to your admin team and ask what they plan to do about it.

c. **Build an internal advocacy team**

Create a simple map showing when, where, and with whom challenges arise. Add questions: What just happened in the day? Look for patterns. Gather a few staff who are ready to speak up. When a harmful decision is made—like cutting supports or punishing students with disabilities—show up together to meetings and speak as a group. Read about disability justice movements and adopt effective language and strategies.

d. **Use art to name what matters.**

Let students make posters or murals about what they want to change in the school. Share stories in morning announcements. Turn the hallway into a space where students name what they care about. Expression is civic presence.

4. Communized Care

a. **Talk about burnout and grief.**

Once a month, hold space for staff to share what's weighing on them—loss, frustration, helplessness, overwhelm. No fixing, no silver linings. Just honesty. Put it on the calendar like any other meeting. Normalize this as part of ethical care, not weakness.

b. **Write crisis plans that don't punish.**

Work with students to make a plan for hard moments: Who should help? What calms them down? What makes things worse? Avoid anything that feels like surveillance or control—listen to kids and believe that they want to do better.

c. **Create "Care Co-Coaching Pods."**

Partner a general education teacher with a paraprofessional or counselor. Meet every few weeks just to ask: "What's hard for you right now?" "How are you trying to show care in your work?" "What do you need?" "What is one skill I can teach you that would help you this week?"

d. **Create weekly movement or quiet time.**

Once a week, let the whole class (or staff team) stretch, dance, lie on the floor, or walk outside together. Let bodies settle. Let silence be okay. That's care, too.

Having now journeyed through this book and this framework, you are more ready to be called to action than you think, not as lone saviors and heroes, but as part of a larger collective force. We are not just educators, we are participants, and leaders, in the struggle. As the radical storyteller and activist Arundhati Roy says, "another world is not only possible, she is on her way" (2014, 144). As we continue to spiral in the vortex that is surely ahead, we have the difficult challenge of recognizing the urgency for this work while remaining calm. Expect exhaustion. Make peace with it, not as something every worker in capitalism deserves, but rather as the fate of every fighter, every revolutionary. And remember that none of us alone can bring about the new world we need. But as a collective, in a community bound by the conviction that the world can and must be radically reimagined, we can reimagine our work and our systems, as many have before us.

REFERENCES

ADA National Network. n.d. https://adata.org/.

ADAPT. n.d. https://adapt.org.

Adichie, Chimamanda Ngozi. 2009. "The Danger of a Single Story." TEDGlobal, Oxford, UK, July. https://www.ted.com/talks/chimamanda_ngozi_adichie_the_danger_of_a_single_story.

American Psychiatric Association. 2013. *Diagnostic and Statistical Manual of Mental Disorders,* Fifth Edition, Text Revision (*DSM*-5-TR). American Psychiatric Association.

Anderson, N., and A. Blue. 2016. "The Hierarchy of Needs Is a Social Product of White Individualism." In "Indigenizing the Curriculum: Reclaiming Indigenous Knowledge Systems." Paper presented at University of Calgary conference.

Apple, Michael. 1990. *Ideology and Curriculum.* 2nd ed. Routledge.

Artiles, Alfredo J., and Stanley C. Trent. 1994. "Overrepresentation of Minority Students in Special Education: A Continuing Debate." *The Journal of Special Education 27* (4): 410–437. https://doi.org/10.1177/002246699402700404.

Artiles, Alfredo J., Robert Rueda, Jesús José Salazar, and Ignacio Higareda. 2002. "English-Language Learner Representation in Special Education in California Urban School Districts." In *Racial Inequity in Special Education*, edited by Daniel J. Losen and Gary Orfield. Harvard Education Press.

Au, Wayne. 2011. *Unequal By Design: High-Stakes Testing and the Standardization of Inequality.* Routledge.

Baldwin, James. 1962. "Letter from a Region in My Mind." *The New Yorker*, November 9. https://www.newyorker.com/magazine/1962/11/17/letter-from-a-region-in-my-mind.

Barrett, Lisa Feldman. 2017. *How Emotions Are Made: The Secret Life of the Brain*. Houghton Miffin Harcourt.

Baynton, Douglas. 2001. "Disability and the Justification of Inequality in American History." In *The New Disability History: American Perspectives*, edited by Paul K. Longmore and Lauri Umansky. New York University Press.

Biesta, Gert. 2010. *Good Education in an Age of Measurement: Ethics, Politics, Democracy*. Routledge.

Blackstock, Cindy. 2011. "The Emergence of the Breath of Life Theory." *Journal of Social Work Values and Ethics* 8 (1): 1–16.

Blackstock, Cindy. 2014. Remarks at the National Indian Child Welfare Association Conference. March.

Boggs, Grace Lee. 2011. *The Next American Revolution: Sustainable Activism for the Twenty-First Century*. University of California Press.

Braidotti, Rossi. 2013. *The Posthuman*. Polity Press.

Brantlinger, Ellen A. 2006. "Conclusion: Whose Labels? Whose Norms? Whose Needs? Whose Benefits?" In *Who Benefits from Special Education? Remediating (Fixing) Other People's Children*, edited by Ellen A. Brantlinger. Routledge.

Bronfenbrenner, Urie. 1979. *The Ecology of Human Development: Experiments by Nature and Design*. Harvard University Press.

Bruer, John T. 1997. "Education and the Brain: A Bridge Too Far." *Educational Researcher* 26 (8): 4–16. https://doi.org/10.3102/0013189X026008004.

Brusaferri, Ludovica et al. 2022. "The Pandemic Brain: Neuroinflammation in Non-Infected Individuals During the COVID-19 Pandemic." *Brain, Behavior, and Immunity* May, 102: 89–97.

Burstow, Bonnie. 2015. *Psychiatry and the Business of Madness: An Ethical and Epistemological Accounting*. Palgrave Macmillan.

Cajete, Gregory. 1986. "*Science: A Native American Perspective.*" PhD diss., International College, Los Angeles.

Cajete, Gregory. 2000. *Native Science: Natural Laws of Interdependence.* Clear Light Publishers.

Cajete, Gregory. 2008. "Seven Orientations for the Development of Indigenous Science Education." In *Handbook of Critical and Indigenous Methodologies*, edited by Norman K. Denzin, Yvonna S. Lincoln, and Linda Tuhiwai Smith. Sage.

CAST. 2024. "Universal Design for Learning Guidelines Version 3.0." Graphic organizer. https://udlguidelines.cast.org.

Cederström, Carl, and André Spicer. 2015. *The Wellness Syndrome.* Polity.

Cipriano, Christina, Sheldon H. Horowitz, and Gabbie Rappolt-Schlichtmann. 2021. "Does Social-Emotional Learning Help Students Who Could Benefit the Most? We Don't Know." *Education Week*, December 6. https://www.edweek.org/leadership/opinion-does-social-emotional-learning-help-students-who-could-benefit-the-most-we-dont-know/2021/12.

Connor, David J., Susan L. Gabel, Deborah J. Gallagher, and Missy Morton. 2008. "Disability Studies and Inclusive Education—Implications for Theory, Research, and Practice. *International Journal of Inclusive Education* 12 (5–6): 441–457. https://doi.org/10.1080/13603110802377482.

Craig, A. D. (Bud). 2015. *How Do You Feel? An Interoceptive Moment with Your Neurobiological Self.* Princeton University Press.

Crotty, Michael. 1998. *The Foundations of Social Research: Meaning and Perspective in the Research Process.* Sage.

Damasio, Antonio. 1994. *Descartes' Error: Emotion, Reason, and the Human Brain.* Putnam Publishing.

Damasio, Antonio. 1999. *The Feeling of What Happens: Body and Emotion in the Making of Consciousness.* Harcourt.

Damasio, Antonio. 2003. *Looking for Spinoza: Joy, Sorrow, and the Feeling Brain.* Harcourt.

Darder, Antonia. 2012. *Culture and Power in the Classroom: Educational Foundations for the Schooling of Bicultural Students.* Routledge.

Darder, Antonia. 2017. *Reinventing Paulo Freire: A Pedagogy of Love*. Routledge.

Davis, Angela Y. 2016. *Freedom Is a Constant Struggle: Ferguson, Palestine, and the Foundations of a Movement*. Haymarket Books.

de Sousa Santos, Boaventura. 2001. "Toward an Epistemology of Blindness: Why the New Forms of 'Ceremonial Adequacy' Neither Regulate nor Emancipate." *European Journal of Social Theory* 4 (3): 251–279. https://doi.org/10.1177/136843101222225109.

de Sousa Santos, Boaventura, ed. 2007. *Cognitive Justice in a Global World: Prudent Knowledges for a Decent Life*. Lexington Books.

de Sousa Santos, Boaventura. 2014. *Epistemologies of the South: Justice Against Epistemicide*. Paradigm Publishers.

Deleuze, Gilles, and Félix Guattari. 1987. *A Thousand Plateaus: Capitalism and Schizophrenia*. Translated by Brian Massumi. University of Minnesota Press.

Dettwyler, Katherine A. 1991. "Can Paleopathology Provide Evidence for 'Compassion'?" *American Journal of Physical Anthropology* 84 (4): 375–84.

Disability Visibility Project. n.d. https://disabilityvisibilityproject.com/.

Dreeben, Robert. 1968. *On What Is Learned in School*. Addison-Wesley.

Duckworth, Sylvia. 2020. "Wheel of Power/Privilege." https://www.flickr.com/photos/sylviaduckworth/50500299716/.

Dudley-Marling, Curt, and Mary Bridget Burns. 2014. "Two Perspectives on Inclusion in the United States." *Global Education Review* 1 (1), 14–31. http://ger.mercy.edu/index.php/ger/article/view/10.

Duncan-Andrade, Jeffrey M. R., and Ernest Morrell. 2008. *The Art of Critical Pedagogy: Possibilities for Moving from Theory to Practice in Urban Schools*. Peter Lang.

Dweck, Carol S. 2008. *Mindset*. Ballantine Books.

Eco, Umberto. 1984. *Postscript to the Name of the Rose*. Harcourt.

Ellenberger, Henri F. 1970. *The Discovery of the Unconscious: The History and Evolution of Dynamic Psychiatry*. Basic Books.

Fischer, Kurt W. 2009. "Mind, Brain, and Education: Building a Scientific Groundwork for Learning and Teacher." *Mind, Brain, and Education* 3 (1): 3–16. https://onlinelibrary.wiley.com/doi/full/10.1111/j.1751-228X.2008.01048.x.

Frances, Allen. 2013. *Saving Normal: An Insider's Revolt Against Out-of-Control Psychiatric Diagnosis, DSM-5, Big Pharma, and the Medicalization of Ordinary Life.* William Morrow.

Frank, Anne. 1995. *The Diary of a Young Girl: The Definitive Edition,* edited by Otto H. Frank and Mirjam Pressler. Translated by Susan Massotty. Bantam.

Frankl, Victor. 1946. *Man's Search for Meaning.* Beacon Press.

Freire, Paolo. 2018. *Pedagogy of the Oppressed.* 50th Anniversary Edition. Translated by Myra Bergman Ramos. Bloomsbury Academic.

Freire, Paolo, and Donaldo P. Macedo. 1995. "A Dialogue: Culture, Language, and Race." *Harvard Educational Review* 65 (3): 377–402.

Fromm, Erich. 1956. *The Art of Loving.* Harper & Row.

Fromm, Erich. 1976. *To Have or To Be?* Harper & Row.

Giroux, Henry A. 1981. *Ideology, Culture, and the Process of Schooling.* Temple University Press.

Gould, Stephen Jay. 1981. *The Mismeasure of Man.* W. W. Norton & Company.

Gouldner, Alvin W. 1970. *The Coming Crisis of Western Sociology.* Basic Books.

Haraway, Donna. 1988. "Situated Knowledges: The Science Question in Feminism and the Privilege of Partial Perspective." *Feminist Studies* 14 (3): 575–599. https://doi.org/10.2307/3178066.

Harding, Sandra. 1986. *The Science Question in Feminism.* Cornell University Press.

Henrich, Joseph. 2020. *The WEIRDest People in the World: How the West Became Psychologically Peculiar and Particularly Prosperous.* Farrar, Straus and Giroux.

Henrich, Joseph, Steven J. Heine, and Ara Norenzayan. 2010. "The Weirdest People in the World?" *Behavioral and Brain Sciences* 33 (2–3): 61–83.

Herman, Judith. 1992. *Trauma and Recovery: The Aftermath of Violence—From Domestic Abuse to Political Terror.* Basic Books.

Heumann, Judith, and Kristen Joiner. 2020. *Being Heumann: An Unrepentant Memoir of a Disability Rights Activist.* Beacon Press.

Hofstede, Geert, Gert Jan Hofstede, and Michael Minkov. 2010. *Cultures and Organizations: Software of the Mind.* 3rd ed. McGraw Hill.

Holt, John. 1964. *How Children Fail.* Pitman.

hooks, bell. 1984. *Feminist Theory: From Margin to Center.* South End Press.

hooks, bell. 1994. *Teaching to Transgress: Education as the Practice of Freedom*. Routledge.

hooks, bell. 2000a. *All About Love: New Visions*. William Morrow.

hooks, bell. 2000b. *Feminism Is for Everybody: Passionate Politics*. South End Press.

Horvath, Adam O., A C Del Re, Christoph Flückiger, and Dianne Symonds. 2011. "Alliance in Individual Psychotherapy." *Psychotherapy* 48 (1): 9–16. https://doi.org/10.1037/a0022186.

Huitt, William. 2007. "Maslow's Hierarchy of Needs." https://www.edpsycinteractive.org/topics/conation/maslow.html.

Immordino-Yang, Mary Helen, and Antonio Damasio. 2007. "We Feel, Therefore We Learn: The Relevance of Affective and Social Neuroscience to Education." *Mind, Brain, and Education* 1 (1): 3–10. https://doi.org/10.1111/j.1751-228X.2007.00004.x.

Jackson, Philip W. 1968. *Life in Classrooms*. Holt, Rinehart, and Winston.

Jung, Carl. 1961. *Memories, Dreams, Reflections*. Pantheon Books.

Jung, Carl. 1979. "Psychological Aspects of the Self." In *The Collected Works of C.G. Jung Part II: Aion: Researches into the Phenomenology of the Self*. Edited and translated by Gerhard Adler and R.F.C. Hull. Princeton University Press.

Kaler-Jones, Cierra. 2020. "When SEL Is Used as Another Form of Policing." Medium, May 7. https://medium.com/@justschools/when-sel-is-used-as-another-form-of-policing-fa53cf85dce4.

Kanafani, Ghassan. 1970. Interview with Richard Carleton for ABC News (Australia). October 16. Rebroadcast September 19, 2024. https://www.abc.net.au/news/2024-09-19/abc-richard-carleton-interviewing-ghassa/104368218.

Kevles, Daniel J. 1995. *In the Name of Eugenics: Genetics and the Uses of Human Heredity*. Harvard University Press.

Kirmayer, Laurence J., and Harry Minas. 2000. "The Future of Cultural Psychiatry: An International Perspective." *Canadian Journal of Psychiatry* 45 (5): 438–46.

Kirsch, Irving, Brett J. Deacon, Tania B. Huedo-Medina, Alan Scoboria, Thomas Moore, and Blair T. Johnson. 2008. "Initial Severity and Antidepressant Benefits: A Meta-Analysis of Data Submitted to the Food and Drug Administration." *PLoS Med* 5 (2): e45. https://doi.org/10.1371/journal.pmed.0050045.

Kirylo, James D. 2013. *Teaching with Purpose: An Inquiry into the Who, Why, and How We Teach*. Rowman & Littlefield.

Kitayama, Shinobu, and Ayse K. Uskul. 2011. "Culture, Mind, and the Brain: Current Evidence and Future Directions." *Annual Review of Psychology* 62 (1): 419–49.

Kliebard, Herbert M. 1999. *Schooled to Work: Vocationalism and the American Curriculum, 1876–1946*. Teachers College Press.

Kliebard, Herbert M. 2004. *The Struggle for the American Curriculum, 1893–1958*. 3rd ed. RoutledgeFalmer.

Konner, Melvin. 2010. *The Evolution of Childhood: Relationships, Emotion, Mind*. Harvard University Press.

Linton, Simi. 1998. *Claiming Disability: Knowledge and Identity*. NYU Press.

Lipman, Pauline. 2004. *High Stakes Education: Inequality, Globalization, and Urban School Reform*. Routledge.

Lipton, Bruce. 2005. *The Biology of Belief: Unleashing the Power of Consciousness, Matter & Miracles*. Mountain of Love/Elite Books.

Longmore, Paul K. 2003. *Why I Burned My Book and Other Essays on Disability*. Temple University Press.

Lorde, Audre. 1984. "Uses of the Erotic: The Erotic as Power." In *Sister Outsider: Essays and Speeches*. Crossing Press.

Lorde, Audre. 2017. "A Burst of Light." In *A Burst of Light and Other Essays*. Ixia Press.

Marche, Stephen. 2022. "The College Essay Is Dead." *The Atlantic*, December 6. https://www.theatlantic.com/technology/archive/2022/12/chatgpt-ai-writing-college-student-essays/672371/.

Mark, Clifton. 2020. "A Belief in Meritocracy Is Not Only False: It's Bad for You." Princeton University Press, June 22. https://press.princeton.edu/ideas/a-belief-in-meritocracy-is-not-only-false-its-bad-for-you?srsltid=AfmBOoo2q8GPAWmdJjPsH8oPo7sRb4xoSy1DvQfSixhgre0qfaVhAxBw.

Maruschak, Laura M., Jennifer Bronson, and Mariel Alper. 2021. "Disabilities Reported by Prisoners: Survey of Prison Inmates, 2016." Bureau of Justice Statistics, March. https://bjs.ojp.gov/library/publications/disabilities-reported-prisoners-survey-prison-inmates-2016.

Maté, Gabor. 2000. *Scattered Minds: The Origins and Healing of Attention Deficit Disorder*. Vintage Canada.

Maté, Gabor. 2011. *In the Realm of Hungry Ghosts: Close Encounters with Addiction.* North Atlantic Books.

Mingus, Mia. n.d. *Leaving Evidence* blog. https://leavingevidence.wordpress.com/about-2/.

Minh-ha, Trinh T. 2009. *Woman, Native, Other: Writing Postcoloniality and Feminism.* Indiana University Press.

Molnar, Alex. 1996. *Giving Kids the Business: The Commercialization of America's Schools.* Westview Press.

Moncrieff, Joanna, Ruth E. Cooper, Tom Stockmann, Simone Amendola, Michael P. Hengartner, and Mark A. Horowitz. 2022. "The Serotonin Theory of Depression: A Systematic Umbrella Review of the Evidence." *Molecular Psychiatry* 28: 3243–256.

Moon, Katie, and Deborah Blackman. 2014. "A Guide to Understanding Social Science Research for Natural Scientists." *Conservation Biology,* 28 (5): 1167-177.

Moon, Katie, and Deborah Blackman. 2017. "A Guide to Ontology, Epistemology, and Philosophical Perspectives for Interdisciplinary Researchers." *Integration and Implementation Insights,* May 2. https://i2insights.org/2017/05/02/philosophy-for-interdisciplinarity/.

Myhre, Kyle Tran. 2017. "How to Explain White Supremacy to a White Supremacist." In *A Love Song, A Death Rattle, A Battle Cry.* Button Publishing.

Newnham, Nicole, and Jim LeBrecht, dirs. 2020. *Crip Camp: A Disability Revolution.* Aired July 23, on Netflix. https://www.youtube.com/watch?v=OFS8SpwioZ4.

Nielsen, Kim E. 2012. *A Disability History of the United States.* Beacon Press.

Norcross, John C., ed. 2011. *Psychotherapy Relationships That Work: Evidence-Based Responsiveness.* 2nd ed. Oxford University Press.

Norcross, John C., and Bruce E. Wampold. 2011. "Evidence-Based Therapy Relationships: Research Conclusions and Clinical Practices." In *Psychotherapy Relationships That Work: Evidence-Based Responsiveness.* 2nd ed, edited by John C. Norcross. Oxford University Press.

Norcross, John C., and Michael J. Lambert. 2018. "Psychotherapy Relationships That Work III." *Psychotherapy* 55 (4): 303–315.

Nunberg, Herman, and Ernst Federn. 1962. *Minutes of the Vienna Psychoanalytic Society, Volume 1 1906–1908*. International Universities Press.

O'Brien, Martin, and Sue Penna. 1999. *Theorizing Welfare: Enlightenment and Modern Society*. Sage Academic Books.

Okun, Tema. n.d. "White Supremacy Culture Characteristics." White Supremacy Culture. https://www.whitesupremacyculture.info/characteristics.html.

Okun, Tema. n.d. "Worship of the Written Word." White Supremacy Culture. https://www.whitesupremacyculture.info/worship-of-written-word.html.

Osgood, Robert L. 2005. *The History of Inclusion in the United States*. Gallaudet University Press.

Paraskeva, João M. 2011. *Conflicts in Curriculum Theory: Challenging Hegemonic Epistemologies*. Palgrave Macmillan.

Piaget, Jean. 1952. *The Origins of Intelligence in Children*. International Universities Press.

Pirayesh, Bibinaz. 2018. "A Critical Interrogation of the Mind, Brain, and Education Movement: Toward a Social Justice Paradigm." PhD diss., Loyola Marymount University, Los Angeles. https://digitalcommons.lmu.edu/cgi/viewcontent.cgi?article=1544&context=etd.

Pollock, Meagan. 2021. "What is Positionality?" *Engineer Inclusion*, March 24. https://engineerinclusion.com/what-is-positionality/.

Priesnitz, Wendy. 2000. *Challenging Assumptions in Education: From Institutionalized Education to a Learning Society*. Alternate Press.

Rathunde, Kevin. 2001. "Toward a Psychology of Potentiality: Maslow's Hierarchy and the Concept of Human Nature." *Journal of Humanistic Psychology* 41 (3):136–60.

Ravilochan, Teju. 2021. "Could the Blackfoot Wisdom That Inspired Maslow Guide Us Now?" Medium, April 4. https://gatherfor.medium.com/maslow-got-it-wrong-ae45d6217a8c.

Rosenberg, Marshall B. 2003. *Nonviolent Communication: A Language of Life*. 2nd ed. PuddleDancer Press.

Roy, Arundhati. 2014. *Capitalism: A Ghost Story*. Verso Books.

Said, Edward W. 1978. *Orientalism*. Pantheon.

Scales, Peter C., and Nancy Leffert. 1999. *Developmental Assets: A Synthesis of the Scientific Research on Adolescent Development*. Search Institute Press.

Shakespeare, Tom. 2006. *Disability Rights and Wrongs*. Routledge.

Simmons, Dena. 2019. "Why We Can't Afford Whitewashed Social–Emotional Learning." *Education Update* 61 (4). https://www.ascd.org/el/articles/why-we-cant-afford-whitewashed-social-emotional-learning.

Sins Invalid. 2019. *Skin, Tooth, and Bone: The Basis of Movement Is Our People*. 2nd ed. Sins Invalid.

Skrtic, Thomas M. 1991. *Behind Special Education: A Critical Analysis of Professional Culture and School Organization*. Love Publishing Company.

Slee, Roger. 1998. "The Politics of Theorising Special Education." In *Theorising Special Education*, edited by Catherine Clark, Alan Dyson, and Alan Millward. Routledge.

Smith, Linda Tuhiwai. 1999. *Decolonizing Methodologies*. Zed Books.

Smith, Robin M., Deborah Gallagher, Valerie Owen, and Thomas M. Skrtic. 2009. "Disability Studies in Education: Guidelines and Ethical Practice." In *Social Justice, Peace, and Environmental Education: Transformative Standards*, edited by Julie Andrzejewski, Marta Baltodano, and Linda Symcox. Routledge.

Spade, Dean. 2020. *Mutual Aid: Building Solidarity During This Crisis (and the Next)*. Verso.

Spencer, Herbert. 1860. *Education: Intellectual, Moral, and Physical*. D. Appleton and Company.

Spencer, Herbert. 1864. *The Principles of Biology*. Williams and Norgate.

Tammet, Daniel. 2011. "Different Ways of Knowing." TED Talk, Long Beach, CA, March. https://www.ted.com/talks/daniel_tammet_different_ways_of_knowing.

Taylor, N. 2019. "Indigenizing Maslow: The Hierarchy of Needs and the Blackfoot World View." *Canadian Journal of Native Education* 41 (1): 31–45.

Temple University Institute on Disabilities. n.d. Disability Rights Timeline. https://disabilities.temple.edu/resources/disability-rights-timeline.

Tuck, Eve, and K. Wayne Yang. 2012. "Decolonization Is Not a Metaphor." *Decolonization: Indigeneity, Education & Society* 1 (1): 1–40.

Wampold, Bruce E. 2001. *The Great Psychotherapy Debate: Models, Methods, and Findings.* Lawrence Erlbaum Associates.

Wang, Leah. 2022. "Chronic Punishment: The Unmet Health Needs of People in State Prisons." Prison Policy Initiative, June. https://www.prisonpolicy.org/reports/chronicpunishment.html#disability.

Wang, Monica L., Alexis Gomes, Marielis Rosa, Phillipe Copeland, and Victor Jose Santana. 2024. "A Systematic Review of Diversity, Equity, and Inclusion and Antiracism Training Studies: Findings and Future Directions." *Translational Behavioral Medicine* 14 (3): 156–71. https://doi.org/10.1093/tbm/ibad061.

Watters, Ethan. 2010. *Crazy Like Us: The Globalization of the American Psyche.* Free Press.

Watters, Ethan. 2013. "We Aren't the World." *Pacific Standard,* February 25. https://psmag.com/social-justice/joe-henrich-weird-ultimatum-game-shaking-up-psychology-economics-53135.

Werner, Emmy E., and Ruth S. Smith. 1992. *Overcoming the Odds: High Risk Children from Birth to Adulthood.* Cornell University Press.

Wong, Julia Carrie. 2025. "Loathe Thy Neighbor: Elon Musk and the Christian Right Are Waging War on Empathy." *The Guardian,* April 8. https://www.theguardian.com/us-news/ng-interactive/2025/apr/08/empathy-sin-christian-right-musk-trump.

World Population Review. 2025. "Individualistic Countries 2025." https://worldpopulationreview.com/country-rankings/individualistic-countries.

Zheng, Lily. 2024. What Needs to Change About DEI—and What Doesn't. *Harvard Business Review,* April 9. https://hbr.org/2024/04/what-needs-to-change-about-dei-and-what-doesnt.

Acknowledgments continued from the copyright page:

Figure 2.3: Wheel of Power, Privilege, and Marginalization by Sylvia Duckworth. Copyright © 2020 by Sylvia Duckworth. Used by permission.

"How to Explain White Supremacy to a White Supremacist" from *A Love Song, A Death Rattle, A Battle Cry* by Kyle Tran Myhre. Copyright © 2017. Courtesy of Button Publishing, Inc.

Figure 3.1A: © Lena Clara/fstop/Corbis/HIP

Figure 3.1B: Google Research and Lichtman Lab renderings by Daniel Berger (Harvard University). Courtesy of the Lichtman Lab, Harvard University, and Google Research.

Figure 6.1: "Four Pillars Framework" by Bibinaz Pirayesh. Copyright © 2018 by Bibinaz Pirayesh. Reproduced by permission of the author.